The Ministry of Labour and National Service

THE NEW WHITEHALL SERIES

is prepared under the auspices of

THE ROYAL INSTITUTE OF PUBLIC ADMINISTRATION

and is edited on its behalf by Sir Robert Fraser, O.B.E.

*The purpose of the series is to provide
authoritative descriptions of the present work
of the major Departments of Central Government*

Already published

THE HOME OFFICE (*reprinted*)

THE FOREIGN OFFICE (*reprinted*)

THE COLONIAL OFFICE

THE MINISTRY OF WORKS

THE SCOTTISH OFFICE

THE MINISTRY OF PENSIONS AND
NATIONAL INSURANCE

THE MINISTRY OF TRANSPORT
AND CIVIL AVIATION

In Preparation

THE MINISTRY OF SUPPLY

THE DEPARTMENT OF INLAND REVENUE

THE ADMIRALTY

THE COMMONWEALTH RELATIONS OFFICE

THE NEW WHITEHALL SERIES

The Ministry of Labour and National Service

SIR GODFREY INCE

G.C.B., K.B.E.

*Formerly Permanent Secretary
to the Ministry*

LONDON · GEORGE ALLEN & UNWIN LTD
NEW YORK · OXFORD UNIVERSITY PRESS INC

FIRST PUBLISHED IN 1960

B60. 2618

PRINTED IN GREAT BRITAIN
in 10 *on* 11 *point Times Roman type*
BY UNWIN BROTHERS LIMITED
WOKING AND LONDON

PREFACE

*

IN deciding the shape of this book, I thought that it would be convenient to the reader to set out in the first two chapters a broad description of the functions of the Ministry of Labour and National Service and the problems with which it has to deal, and to recall the salient features of its history and the way in which it has developed. The following chapters describe each of the Ministry's principal duties in some detail, and in the final chapter I have looked back over the years since the formation of the Ministry and sought to assess the part it has played in the social and industrial history of our time.

I am greatly indebted to many of my former colleagues at the Ministry of Labour and National Service for the very great assistance they have given me in the compilation of this book, particularly in connection with the detailed chapters. I have tried to deal with all the many issues objectively, but if there are any expressions of opinion in the book, they are my own and I accept full responsibility for them.

GODFREY INCE

12th September, 1958

CONTENTS

*

PART I

The Ministry of Labour and National Service

CHAPTER I

The Ministry Today: A General Survey

*

THE Ministry of Labour and National Service, founded in 1916, may perhaps be said to be older than its years in knowledge of the practical handling of problems involving large numbers of people. It has lived through and been vitally concerned with the serious industrial unrest after the First World War, the heavy unemployment of the late 1920's and the 1930's, and the great re-deployment of manpower that was necessary during and after the Second World War. The experience gained from these activities has been woven into the organisation of the Ministry as it now is. Its duties can be divided into four parts:

(1) *Manpower*, embracing the supply of labour to industry and other activities in civil life and to the Forces, and its distribution, training and efficient use, including special responsibility for the employment of young people and the disabled.

(2) *Industrial Relations*, embracing not only the relations between employers and workpeople in matters of wage negotiations and conditions of employment, but also the day-to-day relations between management and workpeople.

(3) *Safety, Health and Welfare*, embracing the physical and environmental conditions of employment and their effect on workpeople.

(4) *International Labour*, embracing the application in an international context of all the problems arising in connection with the above functions of the Department.

It could be contended that all these four functions come within the general term 'manpower' as each of them is related in one form or another to men and their jobs and that essentially the Ministry is one that deals with manpower in all its aspects. While this is true, such a conception would be an over-simplification as many of the problems involved are very different from one another. They do, however, impinge upon each other at a number of points. For example, conditions in factories affect both the supply of labour and labour-management relations; effective training of supervisors may result in improved relations with a firm and shortages and surpluses of labour can have repercussions on wage-rates. Different as the functions are, they have a degree of unity which makes it appropriate that one Department of State should deal with them.

While the Industrial Relations side of the Ministry has played an outstanding part in the industrial history of the country in the last 35 years, the backbone of the Ministry is, and must always be, the Manpower side with its employment service, the main instrument of which is the Employment Exchange service.

Although its functions involve questions of social welfare, the Ministry is essentially an industrial Department. It deals, for the most part, directly with human beings and their individual problems arising from their employment, and this gives it what might be called a humanitarian character which has a profound effect on the staff of the Ministry and on their attitude to the work which they are called upon to perform.

(1) MANPOWER

The term 'manpower' is not confined to what are generally called the workers; it includes all those who are in employment, or might be brought into employment, whether in industry, commerce, the professions or the Armed Forces. Special problems arise in connection with youth employment and with the employment of the disabled, of older workers and of ex-regular members of the Armed Forces. Questions of migration to and from countries overseas and the employment of aliens also raise special issues, while the scarcity of skilled labour and of scientists and technicians presents problems of difficulty and importance if full and effective use of manpower is to be secured. Furthermore, 'manpower' takes the Ministry into the defence field in connection with recruitment for the Armed Forces and the calling up of men for National Service.

The Ministry is concerned with the full and effective use of manpower and the adjustment of its distribution to meet the economic and defence needs of the nation, at the same time taking into account the desires and aspirations of individuals.

'Manpower' and Employment

The maintenance of a high and stable level of employment requires an employment policy based on information relating to the manpower situation nationally and locally and on advice relating to employment aspects of economic policy, of distribution of industry policy and of defence policy.

Distribution of Industry

As will be explained in the next chapter, the Ministry was concerned in the years between the wars with schemes for providing work and, towards the later years of that period, was most closely associated with the carrying out of the policy connected with the Special Areas[1] and the establishment of Trading Estates. In 1944 a major decision of policy was taken to the effect that the Board of Trade should be the Department responsible for general questions of industrial policy and should be the channel of expression of government policy on distribution of industry. The Board of Trade accordingly took over from the Ministry functions in connection with the Special Areas and the development of Trading Estates. It is not an easy matter to determine whether the distribution of industry is more likely to be effectively achieved by an economic Department or a manpower Department. It is largely a question whether production and economic issues or manpower issues are the more important, issues which must obviously vary at different times and in different areas. Wherever the main responsibility lies, the effective carrying out of a policy of distribution of industry must depend on co-operation between the interested Departments.

Under the existing arrangements, it is for the Ministry of Labour to advise the Board of Trade on the manpower position in an area where a firm wishes to establish or enlarge itself. The Ministry also keeps all interested Departments informed of the employment situation in particular districts in order that steps can be taken to increase the employment opportunities in these areas. The Department maintains for this purpose a comprehensive statistical picture, both local and national, of the employment situation.

Local Unemployment

Apart from the effect on employment of the better distribution of industry, the Ministry is concerned with meeting local unemployment by means of vocational training schemes carried out in Government Training Centres to fit workers from declining industries for jobs in expanding industries and by schemes of financial assistance to help the transfer of workers from one area to another (which may involve in some cases transfer to a different occupation). The degree to which this is done naturally varies from time to time according to the needs of the employment situation.

Supply of Manpower

In addition to dealing with problems of unemployment affecting particular areas the Ministry also gives special attention to groups

[1] Now called 'Development Areas'.

of workers who may have particular difficulty in finding suitable employment such as older workers, ex-regular members of the Forces and disabled persons. At the same time, special measures are taken where there is an acute shortage among certain classes, such as technical and scientific workers, and nurses and midwives.

The Employment of Older Workers

A National Advisory Committee,[1] appointed in 1952, advises and assists the Minister in promoting the employment of older people. Following the recommendation of this Committee, the Ministry, basing its policy on the test of capacity not age, endeavours to persuade industry and commerce that all employed men and women who can give effective service should be given the opportunity to continue at work if they so wish. At the same time, the Ministry makes every effort to secure employment for older workers in accordance with their capacity and seeks to persuade employers to revise their engagement and retirement practices, and where necessary their pension schemes.

Resettlement of ex-Regulars

The resettlement in employment of ex-regular members of the Forces has assumed a special importance because of the difficulties of securing sufficient numbers of Regulars. In a time of full employment the Armed Forces have little hope of obtaining the recruits they need unless their conditions, taken generally, compare reasonably— and probably more than reasonably—with those of civilian life. But this is not everything. There is another strong deterrent to recruitment of Regulars in the uncertainty about what may happen on their eventual return to civilian life. This will continue to operate so long as men cannot be certain that after a spell in the Regular Forces they will have a reasonable chance of employment at a level that takes into account their age, experience and ability.

To help overcome this difficulty, the Ministry formed in 1950 an Advisory Council on the Relationship between Employment in the Services and Civilian Life. As a result of their findings and the subsequent approaches by the Ministry to some of the main industrial and commercial undertakings much has been done to ease the

[1] The National Advisory Committee on the Employment of Older Men and Women was wound up in November, 1958, when it was decided that the functions of the Committee in relation to the general policy on the employment of older men and women should be dealt with through the National Joint Advisory Council. An inter-departmental Official Committee was set up to foster research into the problems of employment of older workers.

transfer of ex-Regulars into civilian life. A new situation arose, however, in 1957 when it became known that considerable numbers of Officers and N.C.O.s would have to retire prematurely over the next few years. To deal with this the resettlement machinery was strengthened, a small Resettlement Advisory Board was appointed and Resettlement Committees were set up to cover the various parts of the country.

The Industrial Rehabilitation, Training and Employment of Disabled Persons

The industrial rehabilitation, training and settlement into work of disabled persons is one of the great human problems with which the Department is required to deal. In this work it is guided by a National Advisory Council on the Employment of the Disabled which consists of representatives of employers and trade unions, doctors and other interested people. There are also some 300 Disablement Advisory Committees which have certain statutory functions and assist the Department.

The Ministry derives its powers from the Disabled Persons (Employment) Acts, 1944 and 1958. It registers disabled persons whenever and however handicapped, and administers the scheme under which employers employing 20 or more workers are required to employ a quota of 3 per cent of registered disabled persons and all vacancies in the occupations of passenger electric lift attendant and of car park attendant are reserved for the disabled.

Fifteen industrial rehabilitation centres, some of them residential, are run by the Department. These centres endeavour to fit disabled persons, physically and psychologically, to resume their employment or to start vocational training. The Department provides vocational training for the disabled in the Government Training Centres side by side with non-disabled persons.

To assist and advise disabled persons there is at least one disablement resettlement officer—known as the 'D.R.O.'—at each Employment Exchange. One of his special duties is the placing of disabled persons in employment. In this a man's abilities rather than his disabilities are the important factor. The aim is to place him in the job which enables him, both in his own interests and in those of his employer, to make the fullest possible use of his capacities—in fact, once he is in the right job, the endeavour is always to treat him as no longer handicapped.

To provide employment for severely disabled persons unlikely to get or retain work in industry under ordinary conditions, a Corporation, called Remploy Ltd., has been set up under the Disabled Persons Act. This gives employment in some 90 factories to 6,000

B

severely disabled workers. In addition the Department makes grants to more than 30 voluntary organisations and to local authorities providing facilities for the training and employment of severely disabled persons and the blind.

The Nursing Appointments Service

The Nursing Appointments Service is a good example of the way in which the Ministry has been able to provide a specialised employment service for a particular profession. Started during the war, when the hospitals were working under great strain as the result of inadequate staffs, the Service enabled the Ministry to play an important part in the recruitment and more effective distribution of nurses and midwives. Today there are 166 Nursing Appointments Offices, most of them housed in Employment Exchanges, in charge of officers who have been given a general insight into the working of the nursing profession. Additional guidance is provided by a small number of officers who are themselves state-registered nurses and who have been appointed to give advice on technical nursing matters. Through this Service, the Ministry has been able to help workers in all grades in the profession to find suitable posts, and to give information and advice to girls seeking to enter nursing or the auxiliary medical services.

Youth Employment

In its Youth Employment Service the Ministry is not primarily concerned with increasing the supply of manpower or with augmenting the numbers in particular industries. Rather is it concerned with helping school-leaving boys and girls to find work for which their aptitudes and abilities make them most suitable and with advising them on ways in which they can develop their careers.

Since 1948 the central administration has been run by a Central Youth Employment Executive responsible to the Minister of Labour but including in its membership not only a Chairman and two other members of the Ministry of Labour but also an official from each of the two Education Departments. Local responsibility is divided between the Ministry of Labour and the local education authorities.

The main functions of the service are the provision of vocational guidance for boys and girls about to leave school, placing them in jobs for which they are best suited, and their after-care.

In finding the most suitable job for a school-leaver the guiding principle is the suitability of the job for the individual having regard to his or her ability, aptitude and achievements. While it is important to place young persons in jobs of value to the national interest, it is of greater importance to place them in jobs that are suitable for and satisfying to them. The service is very largely a personal one and its success depends on the youth employment officers, whether they are employed by the Ministry of Labour or by the local education authority.

Distribution of Manpower

In the immediate post-war period the Ministry continued to play a substantial part in the distribution of labour through the control exercised by the Notification of Vacancies Order, and the operation, in the day-to-day placing work of the Employment Exchanges, of preference for under-manned industries and services. These means, for example, contributed largely to the building up of the labour force in coalmining from towards the end of 1951 to the beginning of 1953 by 28,000 and to increasing the labour force in the aircraft industry in 1952 and 1953 by 53,000.

Most of the requirements for manpower are normally met by the day-to-day work of the Employment Exchanges. It is not generally realised to what a great extent this day-to-day work succeeded in building up the labour force in under-manned industries and in securing a substantial redistribution of the labour force. The Employment Exchanges have been able not only to place workers in suitable jobs as speedily as possible but to persuade them to accept jobs of national importance.

Employment Exchange Service

It is sometimes suggested that, with practically no unemployment, the Employment Exchanges are not required. This is a misguided view and shows a lack of appreciation of the facts. A large volume of labour turnover takes place every week—a surprisingly large volume in many cases—and the exchanges are called upon as a continuous and continuing job every day to deal with persons changing their jobs. In a period of full employment it is of special importance that there should be no delay in filling jobs. With a scarcity of labour it is not an easy matter to find the right men and women to fill those vacant jobs which are holding up important work, and it is a much more difficult matter to distribute labour to the best advantage of the country. The work of the exchanges in a period of labour shortage is thus not only more difficult, but more important than at a time when there is plenty of labour available.

Also, full employment has brought another development that has affected the exchanges. Large numbers of workers are not completely satisfied with their jobs. Some of them have ambitions and wish to improve their position; others have long journeys to and from work and wish to work nearer home; and others do not like the atmosphere of their particular factory; there are a hundred and one reasons why workers would like to change their jobs, but do not wish to give up their present jobs until they have secured more suitable ones. The exchanges are being called upon more and more to deal with persons in employment with a view to finding more suitable jobs for them. Much of this work occurs on a Saturday morning which, with the advent of the five-day week in industry, has become one of the busiest days for the exchanges.

Call-up for National Service

On the National Service side of 'manpower' the Department has had the task of registering, medically examining and calling up young men for the Forces. Involved in this is the administration of the arrangements connected with postponement of call-up on account of individual hardship, deferment of call-up in the national interest, and conscientious objection. Special arrangements exist for the allocation of skilled men to corresponding trades in the Services. The procedure of call-up works smoothly in complete co-operation with the Service Departments; it aims at equity of treatment of all classes of the community, at the same time ensuring that there will be no undue hardship in any particular cases.

The Government are now planning on the basis that no more men will be called up after 1960. Until that time reliance is being placed as far as practicable on men whose call-up had been deferred, supplemented as necessary by younger men. The Department has to administer this scheme and deal with the many questions which are bound to arise as National Service draws to an end.

(2) INDUSTRIAL RELATIONS

For the Ministry of Labour and National Service the term 'industrial relations' includes the determination of rates of wages and conditions of employment both by voluntary negotiation and by machinery established by statute, the promotion of constitutional machinery within industries for settling trades disputes, and the prevention and settlement of disputes by way of conciliation and arbitration. Used in the widest sense, it also includes the promotion of good human relations in industry.

In the sense in which it is more generally used in industry today the term 'industrial relations' is regarded as covering the relations that arise from the negotiation of wages and conditions of employment between employers and workpeople—negotiations which take place between trade unions on the one hand and employers' organisations or individual employers on the other.

Industrial relations are thus based on organisation. In contrast, 'human relations' are between human beings acting as individuals or as unorganised groups—they are between man and man. They therefore concern the relations between management and workers in the individual industrial unit and involve questions of personnel management, safety, health and welfare.

It is perhaps unfortunate that industrial relations and human relations have come to be regarded as two separate things for they are very much bound up together. To a great extent one is complementary to the other. Good industrial relations are certainly a necessary background to the full development of good human relations in the individual firms in an industry.

Settlement of Disputes on Wages and Conditions of Employment

Wages and conditions of employment are normally settled by collective bargaining—by voluntary negotiation between employers or employers' associations on the one side and the trade unions on the other. In many industries there is agreed machinery for dealing with claims relating to wages and conditions, and also for dealing with disputes if and when they arise: this machinery frequently provides for conciliation and for reference to arbitration.

It is the traditional policy of the Government that industry should be given the fullest encouragement to settle its own affairs, and that the State should take action only when there is no effective bargaining machinery in an industry or when negotiations through an industry's machinery have broken down. This general policy has been written into all legislation in this sphere.

There can be little doubt that this policy has been eminently successful. It was allowed to operate throughout the Second World War—a period of great stress and strain during which wages never got out of control in this country. The United Kingdom was, in fact, practically the only country in the world that did not find it necessary to impose some form of wages control during the war.

The Ministry has certain powers under the Conciliation Act, 1896, and the Industrial Courts Act, 1919, enabling it to take action by way of conciliation and by providing facilities for arbitration for the purpose of helping employers and workpeople to reach settlements when disputes are threatening the peace of the industry. It also has power to appoint a court of inquiry to ascertain and report to Parliament the facts and circumstances of a dispute. In addition it has responsibility under certain other Acts,[1] notably the

[1] The Catering Wages Act, 1943, was repealed as from 30th May, 1959, by the Terms and Conditions of Employment Act, 1959, which brought the catering industry within the field of the Wages Councils Acts.

Wages Councils Acts and the Catering Wages Act, 1943, to establish statutory machinery for the negotiation of wages and conditions of employment in unorganised and low-paid industries, where there are no adequate wage-regulating arrangements.

Thus the Ministry has a twofold duty. In the first place, in those industries where there is no machinery of negotiation and no constitutional procedure for dealing with disputes, it is the Department's task to encourage the employers and the unions to agree to set up such machinery, so that if and when difficulties arise there is agreed procedure for dealing with them. Secondly, if no such machinery has in fact been established in an industry or if no settlement of a dispute has been effected by existing machinery of negotiation, it is the task of the Department to endeavour to secure a settlement by way of conciliation. It is also, however, a very important part of the Department's task to prevent, by early and timely advice, incipient disputes from coming to a head.

There is one important fact that seems often to be lost sight of by the parties to a dispute, namely, that unless they are prepared to let a third party—an arbitrator—settle it for them, they themselves must settle it. The Department has no power to impose a settlement and it would lose its position as a conciliation authority if it once attempted to do so. It must at all times remain impartial and endeavour to lead the parties to their own agreement.

In recent years there has been a change of attitude both in industry and among the general public about intervention in trade disputes by the Department. In the inter-war period, the Department did not normally intervene unless invited by one or other of the parties to a dispute to do so. The policy was one of caution—of 'later rather than sooner'. Nowadays there seems to be a general expectation that the Department will intervene immediately a dispute arises and should in fact do so. One of the reasons for this is that any serious interruption of production can quickly affect the country's economic position and react adversely on our overseas balance of trade. There is a danger in too early intervention for it is inclined to encourage lack of care in the expectation that the Department will extricate those concerned from the results of their irresponsibility. To delay intervention in order to give the parties in dispute time to reflect on the results of their action and for public opinion to show itself—and public opinion has a strong influence on disputes—may make intervention, when it does take place, much more effective. In fact, the timing of intervention is of great importance in dealing with trade disputes, and the right time can only be determined by a close knowledge of the facts. It is still the case that premature intervention may well prolong a dispute.

In any case, it is a cardinal principle not to intervene unless and until the agreed machinery for settling disputes in an industry has been fully used and the means for settlement through this machinery has been exhausted.

The Department is frequently urged to intervene in 'unofficial' stoppages and criticised for not doing so. These are stoppages where men have ceased work without the authority of their union or contrary to its instructions and the men are often led by self-appointed leaders. Intervention by the Department in these cases must inevitably have the effect of undermining the authority of the accredited representatives of the union and of giving recognition to the unofficial leaders. It is for the union itself to deal with its own members and the role of the Department is to keep in touch with the union and to be available to give any help or advice that the union may require.

The role of the Minister himself in trade disputes is not easy to describe. As special qualities are needed by those who have to carry out the work of conciliation and as, when a dispute exists, it absorbs the whole time of a conciliator, the work is allocated to the Chief Industrial Commissioner. The Permanent Secretary rarely appears at negotiations, but is available for consultation at all times. It is the job of the Chief Industrial Commissioner and his officers, acting of course always on behalf of the Minister, to carry on the negotiations for a settlement—negotiations which can be most exacting, frequently frustrating and at all times difficult—at the same time keeping the Minister and the Permanent Secretary fully informed of the course of events. It is when the Chief Industrial Commissioner has done everything possible to obtain a settlement and has not fully succeeded, or there has been a breakdown in the negotiations, that the Minister is brought in, and by virtue of his Ministerial position and the weight of the authority he holds, his intervention can at that stage often be decisive.

It is the policy of the Department to try to persuade the parties to a dispute to reach a settlement by negotiation. If, however, this is not possible the Department endeavours to persuade them to refer the dispute for settlement to one of the forms of voluntary arbitration. An arbitration award is not legally binding on the parties, but the fact that both parties have voluntarily agreed to go to arbitration implies acceptance of the decision of the tribunal. There is a long-standing tradition in this country that arbitration awards are accepted, a tradition that has only been broken on the rarest occasions. If it were not so, the whole system of arbitration would be undermined.

Many industries include in their agreed negotiating machinery provision for the reference of disputes to arbitration. There is, however, no general agreement in industry about this. It is often suggested that provisions of this kind are a disguised attempt to take away the right to strike; and that they weaken the machinery of joint negotiation as neither side will negotiate seriously knowing that arbitration is in the background. On the other hand, it is pointed out that this in fact has not happened in those industries having such a provision, and that, if employers and workers in industry were to agree that all unresolved differences should be referred to some form of arbitration, a valuable safeguard would be introduced against hasty action and both sides would have the assurance of an impartial judgment in their disputes. Indeed, it is suggested by some that the assurance of ultimate arbitration might in many cases help to avoid the need for arbitration and that voluntary arrangements providing for unsettled difficulties to be submitted to arbitration would introduce a further element of stability into industrial relations. Although there are differences of view in industry on this important issue, it is generally agreed that the aim is to develop the collective bargaining system so that all wages and conditions will be determined by the process of voluntary negotiations and all disputes settled by constitutional machinery.

Compulsory arbitration has never been liked in industry. The trade unions in particular seem to dislike it in principle, but at the same time resort to it more frequently than employers. Under the Industrial Disputes Order, 1951,[1] which modified the war-time Order prohibiting strikes and lock-outs, the system of arbitration at the instance of only one party has been continued. It is, however, not part of the permanent structure of industrial relations and the Government has undertaken that it will be reviewed at any time at the request of either side of industry. The surprising thing is that it has survived so long. It is one of the illogicalities with which people disagree in theory but find useful in practice.

The Nationalised Industries present some special features in connection with industrial relations. By statute they are required to set up negotiating machinery and have done so. This machinery is not, however, precisely the same for all of them. In coalmining, for example, it provides, if no agreement is reached by negotiation, for wages and conditions to be settled by an arbitrator whose decision is to be final. In railways, the machinery similarly provides for arbitration, but it is not laid down that the parties are required

[1] The Industrial Disputes Order, 1951, was revoked in December, 1958. Later, a subsidiary feature of the Order, relating to the observance of industrial agreements, became part of permanent law in the spring of 1959 (Section 8 of the Terms and Conditions of Employment Act, 1959).

to accept the award as final and indeed it has not always been accepted. The non-acceptance of such an award, however, does run counter to the general practice in industry and is damaging to the voluntary system of arbitration.

The work of the Department in dealing with disputes frequently attracts much prominence in the Press. This is inevitable, particularly when the prevention of a stoppage of work or the settlement of a strike may have a profound effect on the economy of the country. But the Department's greatest value lies, not in the settlement of a few spectacular disputes, but in the unobtrusive influence which it exercises from day to day through its conciliation officers and which over the years has brought an increasing spirit of harmony into industry.

Wages Boards and Councils

As has already been mentioned, another branch of the Ministry's industrial relations work deals with the establishment of Wages Boards and Councils for those unorganised and low-paid industries where there is no adequate wage-regulating machinery, and with the work of the Wages Inspectorate. The proposals of the Wages Boards and Councils for rates and conditions are given statutory effect by Wages Regulations Orders made by the Minister, whose confirmation of the proposals in this way is intended to be a safeguard for the public, but which in practice he cannot withhold, except on technical grounds, without raising a storm of protest.

It is the policy of the Government to encourage the development of voluntary negotiating machinery in industries for which Wages Councils are established so that state intervention will not be required indefinitely. Since the Wages Councils Act was passed in 1945 only five Wages Councils have been abolished and replaced by a voluntary wage-regulating body. This is very slow progress largely due to the difficulties experienced by the trade unions in organising workpeople in the industries concerned. The day when all Wages Councils are replaced by voluntary wage-regulating bodies and thus all wages and conditions settled by voluntary negotiation still seems a long way ahead.

The Wages Inspectorate of the Ministry is also responsible for the enforcement of the Catering Wages Act, 1943,[1] and the Baking Industry (Hours of Work) Act, 1954, which restricts night-baking in the industry. The Ministry has, however, no responsibility for the work of the two Agricultural Wages Boards for England and Wales, and Scotland; this lies with the Ministry of Agriculture,

[1] Repealed by the Terms and Conditions of Employment Act, 1959, which converted Catering Wages Boards into Wages Councils.

Fisheries and Food and the Department of Agriculture for Scotland, respectively.

Human Relations

The work of the Ministry in the field of human relations in industry is included as part of its industrial relations work, although it is closely linked to the Department's activities in the safety, health and welfare fields. For humanitarian reasons, good relations between management and workers are an end in themselves—they are a direct contribution to human happiness and to peace in industry; at the same time they are of great importance in making more efficient use of the country's manpower—one of the essential factors in securing increased productivity. On the one hand there is the social need to try to make a man's work a satisfying and satisfactory part of his life and, on the other, there is the urgency of the call for increased production and productivity to safeguard the economic position of the country.

Formerly it was considered that good relations in an industrial undertaking depended on paying adequate wages and providing good conditions of employment. Today fair wages and good conditions, being for the most part determined by collective bargaining, tend to be taken for granted and the development of good human relations starts from that point. The success of these depends not only on the provision of welfare and other similar services but also, and perhaps mainly, on the way in which day-to-day matters are handled over a long period. The building up of mutual confidence and understanding between those who give and those who take orders in an industrial undertaking is not an easy process. The fact is there is no short cut to success in what is probably one of the most important tasks in a free society.

Through the change in the structure of industry since the turn of the century, management may have become more impersonal in their relations with workpeople and therefore have become less aware of their needs and desires. If good human relations are to be restored many students of these matters take the view that management must take pains to study their workpeople and to understand their needs. Everyone wishes to be treated with justice, but beyond that is the deep desire to be recognised as a responsible human being.

A number of techniques, such as joint consultation, improved methods of communication, and the dissemination of information throughout the undertaking have been developed for these purposes, but they have met with varying results. They are not, of course, by any means of universal application throughout industry but, where they have been applied with thoroughness and understanding, there is evidence to suggest that they can succeed in securing confidence between management and workpeople and thus obtain the right attitude of mind towards their mutual problems which will lead to the establishment of good human relations.

The Ministry, which is concerned both with the humanitarian and the economic aspects of improved human relations in industry, provides a Personnel Management Advisory Service whose function is to give practical help and guidance to firms wishing to set up a personnel department, to personnel officers in industry, and to the smaller and medium-sized firms without a personnel department. Most of the larger firms in industry have very efficient personnel departments but when it is remembered that only about 3 per cent of the 200,000 factories in the country employ more than 250 people, it will be seen that there is a vast field to be covered. From their wide experience of personnel management and their collective observation of the causes of failure and success of various techniques in individual firms, the Department's officers are able to give sound guidance and to exercise an influence out of proportion to their numbers. They work in close co-operation with the professional bodies operating in this field of social and industrial welfare, and during the few years they have been operating have fulfilled the hopes of Mr Ernest Bevin in adding to the sum of human happiness in industry.

(3) SAFETY, HEALTH AND WELFARE

The Ministry's present duties for safety, health and welfare arose mainly out of the transfer to the Ministry from the Home Office in June, 1940, of the administration of the Factories Acts. These duties involve the maintenance and where possible the improvement in the standards of safety, health and welfare. They are carried out both by administrative action and by inspection. The administrative function is discharged in close consultation with the Factory Inspectorate and in co-operation with employers and workers and their organisations. The duties of the Inspectors, who have wide powers and considerable freedom as to the way in which they can perform them, are to see that the requirements of the Factories Acts and the various Regulations made under them are effectively carried out. Their basic approach is to help the factory occupier to comply with the law and to run his factory on the lines of the best modern practice.

The field to be covered is very wide, including safety at work, the prevention of industrial disease, the hours of employment of women and young persons, and such health and welfare measures that cover cleanliness, overcrowding, ventilation, heating, lighting, rest facilities and the provision of first aid. To assist in the development of industrial health services in workplaces covered by the Factories Acts, the Minister is advised by the Industrial Health Advisory Committee. Probably protection against accidents and industrial disease and the development of industrial health services in factories are among the most important of these at a time of full employment affecting as they do absenteeism, time off from work and other issues concerned with the efficient use of manpower. In this connection the specialist medical, engineering, chemical and electrical branches play an effective part in studying the medical and technical aspects of occupational health and safety problems and methods of dealing with them.

It is also the task of the Ministry to keep abreast of the new hazards which arise from the great industrial developments taking place, for example, in the fields of automation, electronics and atomic energy and to ensure that, through the Inspectorate, management and workers take the measures needed to counter them.

(4) INTERNATIONAL LABOUR

The Ministry's functions are not confined to dealing with labour matters in Great Britain only. Many of the problems are common to many countries, and knowledge of the way in which these problems are dealt with in other countries is often of the greatest value. Moreover, Great Britain, being an industrial country of long experience and tradition, is able to provide other countries with information that can assist them in dealing with their labour problems. Exchange of information on all aspects of labour matters is invaluable. This is mainly done through the various international organisations, particularly the International Labour Organisation, and through the Labour Attachés at British Embassies abroad.

By virtue of its knowledge and experience of labour matters and the consistently active part it has played in the affairs of the International Labour Organisation since it was established in 1919, the Department exercises much influence at the General Conference, in the Governing Body of the International Labour Office and in the various Committees of the Organisation. Much of the day-to-day work calls for frequent consultation with the Organisation as well as with other branches of the Ministry and other Government Departments.

Labour Attachés, who form part of the staff of the Diplomatic Mission and are normally officers of the Ministry of Labour, advise the Head of the Mission on all branches of labour matters and report major developments in the labour and industrial fields of the country to which they are assigned. They meet requests from official, trade union or employers' representatives for information on conditions in the United Kingdom, or upon British policy and practice on a wide range of labour and social questions. Their reports keep the Ministry at home informed of labour and social legislation and administrative practices in other countries and make possible comparisons with the British parallels. They also provide a valuable source of information on current trends and developments on labour and social matters which may be the subject of consideration in the International Labour Organisation or other international bodies.

There are 18 Labour Attachés in posts at Diplomatic Missions in North, Central and South America, Europe, the Middle East and Asia. In some cases they have responsibility for neighbouring countries as well as the country in which they are stationed, and in all 52 countries are covered. This service has proved of great value both to the Heads of Missions and to the Department at home. Not the least valuable results of the work of the Labour Attachés have been the better understanding of the British point of view and the fund of goodwill towards this country which they have helped to create in the minds of important and influential elements in foreign countries which, without the assistance of the Labour Attaché, are not easily reached.

The Ministry's Overseas Department has a wide range of activities, dealing with all international labour issues and with the questions of migration of labour to and from this country and with the employment of aliens under the Aliens Order, 1953. This wide scope takes the Department into all the activities of the Ministry's work at home.

(5) CO-OPERATION WITH INDUSTRY AND ADVISORY COUNCILS

In carrying out its many functions and dealing with such a wide variety of subjects, some of them of a general and many of them of a technical nature, the Ministry follows two complementary principles. First of all, it endeavours to carry with it the willing co-operation of employers and workpeople. Secondly, as it clearly cannot possess all the knowledge required to deal with the problems with which it is faced, it seeks the assistance of those who can supply that knowledge. As a result, the Ministry is helped by a series of Advisory Councils—Councils which are not façades but whose help and advice is earnestly sought and used.

Among the most important of these is the National Joint Advisory Council, consisting of representatives of the British Employers' Confederation, the Trades Union Congress and the Nationalised Industries, which advises the Minister on all issues of major policy—advice which, of course, he is free to accept or reject. The Council meets quarterly, but a special meeting can be called at any time. A Committee of the Council—called the Joint Consultative Committee—meets to consider issues referred to it by the Council, to whom it reports. The Minister, or in his absence, the Parliamentary Secretary, presides over the Council.

To advise the Minister on matters of employment policy relating to women there is a Women's Consultative Committee which meets under the chairmanship of the Parliamentary Secretary; the membership is composed of women prominent in public affairs who, although appointed in a personal capacity, collectively reflect the views of the principal organisations in which women's interests find expression.

Among the other Advisory Councils which help the Department in its specialist problems—most of which have already been mentioned in connection with the services with which they are concerned —are the National Advisory Council on the Employment of the Disabled, the National Youth Employment Council, the National Advisory Committee on the Employment of Older Men and Women,[1] the Resettlement Advisory Board, the Industrial Health Advisory Committee and the Cost of Living Advisory Committee. In some cases the Minister is Chairman, whilst in three cases independent persons have been appointed. The great volume of advice and knowledge emanating from these Councils is of immense value to the Ministry in carrying out its tasks. In addition, the Department is assisted locally by a system of Local Employment Committees, many of which have a Women's Sub-Committee; Disablement Advisory Committees; and Youth Employment Committees. Resettlement Committees dealing with the resettlement of ex-Regulars function in each of the Department's administrative regions.

[1] See Footnote on page 16.

CHAPTER II

History and Development of the Ministry

*

THE first chapter has surveyed the Ministry's current functions. This chapter gives an account of the Ministry's origins and background and of some of the extremely important phases through which it has passed together with a description of how its functions came into being and how they have been developed.

(1) BACKGROUND AND ORIGINS

The Nineteenth Century

Although the Ministry is comparatively young, its roots lie in a much earlier period—in the years of the industrial revolution and of the growth of industrialism in the nineteenth century. The Elizabethan and later labour laws had largely fallen into disuse at the beginning of the industrial revolution towards the end of the eighteenth century and at the turn of the century the workpeople had little or no protection of any sort as factories using steam and machinery began to develop rapidly. It was an age dominated by *laissez-faire* theories in the economic field and although industrial and social evils soon became manifest, the recognition that state intervention would be required to grapple with these evils was slow to develop. Many new problems arose from the exploitation of child labour, the relations between masters and men, the conditions of employment, the safety, health and welfare of workers in factories and mines, of under-payment and 'sweating', and of unemployment and its relief. These problems could not be ignored and the State found itself forced increasingly to take action.

The first State intervention began in 1802 with the passing of the Health and Morals of Apprentices Act. This Act sought to protect apprentices by limiting the number of hours worked each day and abolishing night-work, and by providing for religious teaching, suitable sleeping accommodation, clothing, and for cleanliness and ventilation in the factories. Protection was extended in 1819 to child labour in cotton factories, the employment of children under 9 years of age being prohibited and the daily working hours of those above that age being limited to 12. Provisions of a similar kind were extended in 1833 to textile factories generally and applied to young persons under 18 years of age as well as to children. Night-work was prohibited and inspectors were appointed to enforce the law for the first time. The latter was an important event as it represented the first step in state intervention by officials to enforce the law and was the beginning of the Factory Inspectorate as we know it today.

From 1845 the regulation of hours of employment of women and young persons and provisions for the safety, health and welfare of workpeople were gradually extended until by 1878 all factories and workshops were concerned.

Another protection of a different kind was provided by the Truck Act, 1831, which made the wages of workmen payable only in the current coin of the realm and prohibited the whole or the part payment of wages in food, drink, clothes or any other articles.

While these important protective and regulative measures were being carried out, other equally important events affecting the lives of the workpeople were taking place. By English common law combinations, whether of masters or men, were regarded as conspiracies in restraint of trade and therefore illegal. As a result of the employment of large numbers of workmen in factories, trade unions in the form of secret societies had become numerous and active by the beginning of the nineteenth century and in order to deal summarily with the situation an Act was passed in 1800 under which all persons combining with others to advance their wages or decrease the quantity of their work were liable to conviction and imprisonment. Following a period of much unrest consequent upon the introduction of steam and machinery into the factories and a great increase in the number of workpeople, the Anti-Combination Laws were abolished in 1824. The Repeal Act was followed by an Amending Act the following year which, while it did not confer the same degree of freedom as the Act of 1824, did give a measure of protection to societies for the purpose of regulating wages and hours of employment. This marked the beginning of the growth of trade union organisation. To begin with many new unions were formed, but owing to depression in trade and other factors there were many set-backs. From the middle of the century slow progress was made, and it was not until the Trade Union Act, 1871, was passed that trade unions were no longer illegal at common law because of their purpose in restraint of trade, and their rapid growth took place.

The growth of trade union organisation in turn stimulated the development of employers' organisations. By the middle of the nineteenth century many unions had secured recognition by employers and agreements governing relationships between them and employers began to make headway. This was the beginning of the system of collective bargaining. As organisation of employers and workers developed during the latter half of the century, negotiations for the determination of wages and conditions of employment became of increasing importance and arrangements for settling disputes on a widespread basis became necessary. In view of the effect on industry of industrial disputes a Royal Commission was set up in 1891 which made a number of recommendations, most of which were incorporated in the Conciliation Act, 1896. This Act for the first time enabled the State to provide facilities by way of conciliation, inquiry and arbitration in order to assist representatives of employers and workers to settle their differences.

Thus, in the course of the nineteenth century the attitude of the State changed considerably. The idea that labour relations and working conditions should be left to the unfettered operation of economic forces became increasingly unacceptable. As a consequence, while labour relations continued to be regarded as matters that should be dealt with on the basis of industrial self-government, it became necessary to provide a proper legal framework and to legislate for state action to assist industry in cases of difficulty. At the same time, so far as the protection of the working conditions of the workpeople was concerned, the attitude of the State became one of benevolent intervention. This made the establishment of a State Department responsible for labour matters inevitable.

The Present Century

With the growing influence of the Parliamentary Committee of the Trades Union Congress, the forerunner of the Trades Union Congress General Council, and the rise of the Labour Party, the early years of the present century saw still more labour legislation involving the intervention of the State: the Unemployed Workmen Act, 1905, under which 19 offices (forerunners of the Labour Exchanges) were set up in London by a special Committee under Mr William (now Lord) Beveridge; the Labour Exchanges Act of 1909, under which the first State Labour Exchanges (as they were originally called) were set up for the purpose of bringing workers seeking work into touch with employers requiring workers; the Trade Boards Act of 1909, which established wage-fixing machinery in certain 'sweated' industries for the purpose of determining statutory minimum wages; the Education (Choice of Employment) Act, 1910, under which a youth employment service began to be developed by giving local education authorities in England and

C

Wales power to set up vocational guidance schemes for boys and girls leaving school and for the Board of Trade to do so through the Labour Exchanges in those areas where the education authority did not avail itself of these powers; and with the National Insurance Act, 1911, a start was made with a scheme for insuring workers against unemployment and ill-health. It was this industrial and social legislation in the early years of the twentieth century, together with the Old Age Pensions Act of 1908, that laid the foundations of the welfare state as we know it today; and a step nearer to the establishment of the Ministry of Labour.

Responsibility for labour matters was shared by a number of Departments. While the protective legislation relating to factories was enforced, as already explained, by inspectorates under the Home Office, and the relief of distress was dealt with by the Local Government Board, the main responsibility for administering labour legislation, although this was comparatively light in volume, fell to the Labour Department of the Board of Trade. The presentation to Parliament of all matters relating to labour by one Minister and the administration of all labour legislation by one Department of State came to be the expressed wish of the Parliamentary Committee of the Trades Union Congress and as early as 1894 four trade union representatives on the Royal Commission on Labour, 1891–94, presented a Minority Report recommending among other things the centralisation under one Minister of Cabinet rank and in one Government Department of all legislation relating to labour. It was, however, not until over 20 years later that a separate Ministry of Labour was created and when this took place towards the end of 1916 it was due primarily to the exigencies of the First World War.

Outbreak of War

It was not long after the beginning of the war in 1914 that problems of manpower became of great importance. There was considerable competition for the limited supply of labour available and as the problems became more difficult and complex it became clear that some co-ordinating and centralised authority was necessary. Accordingly, in 1916, two steps were taken. The first was the appointment on a wartime basis of a Director-General (later Minister) of National Service to deal with labour supply policy and labour priorities; the second was the appointment on a permanent basis of a Minister of Labour to take over the functions of the Labour Department of the Board of Trade, greatly extended as they were in wartime, and, in addition, to take over from the Ministry of Munitions the handling of the work of conciliation and arbitration in labour disputes involving munition workers, and generally to endeavour to promote good labour-management relations in industry.

The Ministry of Labour

It cannot be said that the birth of the Ministry took place at a very auspicious moment. In the early months of the war there were no definite arrangements for the allocation of manpower and the Government had to proceed by trial and error, using more than one Department for the purpose. A number of schemes were devised, none of them wholly successful, until, early in 1917, a Minister of National Service was appointed, replacing the Director-General appointed in the previous year, with central authority for the control of labour for both civilian and military purposes. During these years, the Labour Exchanges, which were only beginning to get into working order at the outbreak of war, were required to adapt their machinery to mobilise men and women for war work. They took a large share of the work of the mobilisation of the reserve of labour, arranged the transfers of thousands of workers from civilian to war work and recruited ever-increasing numbers of women for work in munitions, on the land and in the Women's Services. In addition, their work in connection with unemployment insurance was nearly doubled in 1916 when the scheme was extended to cover men and women engaged in the production of munitions and war materials.

It was into this complex situation that the new Department was thrust. Fortunately for the Department, it was not at once given all the duties and responsibilities that could properly have been assigned to it and the Ministry of National Service continued to function in co-operation with it. But its duties were quickly enlarged. On the one hand, it was required to prepare plans for the resettlement of ex-Servicemen and women and of civilian war-workers, and on the other, it had to give urgent attention to the problems arising from the strained relations between employers and workers in industry. The Ministry was born in a crisis and for some years proceeded from one crisis to another.

(2) THE INTER-WAR YEARS

Employment and Unemployment between the Wars

During the inter-war years the economic position of the country underwent many changes. Immediately following the end of the First World War, there was a period of boom. This enabled the plans for demobilisation and resettlement to mature, but before they could become fully effective the economic situation began to deteriorate and unemployment to increase. This went on throughout the 1920's, and in the early 1930's the number of unemployed reached nearly 3 million, and mass unemployment became the dominant issue before the country. The climax was passed in 1933, but from the onset of heavy unemployment in the early 1920's until the outbreak of the Second World War in 1939, unemployment remained at a high level. One of the major tasks of the Ministry in these interwar years, therefore, was that of relieving unemployment.

The main instruments for this purpose were twofold—the making of grants to subsidise schemes of work in order to increase employment and the payment of money to those unemployed.

In order to encourage local authorities and public utility companies, by offers of financial assistance, to undertake public works in advance of immediate need and thus provide employment, an Unemployment Grants Committee was set up in 1920 at the onset of the trade depression. The Department was required to certify that serious unemployment existed in the areas applying to the Committee for grants and later became the grant-making authority. Also, in order to induce workers to transfer from areas of heavy unemployment to other parts of the country where prospects were better, grants or loans were made by the Department to those willing to transfer.

These measures only provided a limited alleviation in the employment situation and in 1934 measures were initiated with a view to work being taken to the areas of exceptionally high unemployment. Under the Special Areas (Development and Improvement) Act, 1934, two Commissioners were established, one for England and Wales responsible to the Minister of Labour and one for Scotland responsible to the Secretary of State for Scotland, with wide powers to experiment on schemes designed to facilitate the introduction of new industries into what were called the 'Special Areas'; these areas were those parts of the country with exceptionally heavy unemployment and had previously been called 'Depressed Areas'. An amending Act in 1937 gave authority for factory premises and financial inducements to be provided to industrial firms to encourage them to open works in these areas: this was the beginning of the Trading Estates. At the same time local authorities were encouraged by exchequer grants to undertake additional works for the improvement of public utility services. These measures provided the first example of a state policy of 'taking the work to the workers' and were the forerunner of the present scheme for the distribution of industry.

A number of other employment schemes were established during the inter-war years, some connected with the aftermath of the war and some for the purpose of providing more work. For the purpose of assisting disabled ex-servicemen to secure employment, a King's National Roll Scheme was set up under which firms employing a percentage—normally 5 per cent—of such men were given preference in the allocation of government contracts. The Government Instructional Factories opened in 1916 to train the disabled of the First World War were used during the inter-war years to combat heavy unemployment, for example in the Depressed Areas.

For professional and business training for ex-Servicemen a scheme was administered by a newly created Appointments Service of the Ministry, and a Civil Liabilities (Resettlement) Scheme provided grants to discharged and demobilised officers and men to enable them to re-establish themselves in civilian life. In order to devise and carry out special schemes of work and training for unemployed women or for those whose capacities or opportunities had been injuriously affected by conditions arising out of the war, a Central Committee on Women's Training and Employment, established during the war to deal with schemes for the training and employment of women, was reappointed at the beginning of 1920. All these schemes made modest contributions in dealing with the problems of the unemployed.

Direct relief to the unemployed was made by out-of-work donation—'the dole'—or by unemployment benefit. The out-of-work donation scheme, introduced at the end of the First World War, was an interim measure financed by the Exchequer and administered through the Employment Exchanges. It covered practically the whole working population and remained in operation until 1922, by which time a more comprehensive scheme of unemployment insurance, covering most manual workers and also non-manual workers earning not more than £250 a year, and bringing about 8 million new contributors into the scheme, had become operative following the passing of the Unemployment Insurance Act, 1920.

During the war, when unemployment had almost disappeared, the Unemployment Insurance Fund had accumulated a balance of over £20 million but, with the wide extension of the Unemployment Insurance Scheme and mounting unemployment, this sum was soon used up and various expedients, including borrowing, were adopted and a substantial part of the financial burden was transferred to the Exchequer. In addition, modifications were made in the coverage and benefits of the scheme—there were no fewer than 16 amending Acts between 1920 and 1934.

Following the recommendations of a Royal Commission, legislation was passed which aimed at a permanent self-supporting scheme of unemployment insurance (with a state contribution equal to that of an employer and an employee) and provided for a scheme of unemployment assistance for those outside insurance or who had exhausted their right to insurance benefit. The Minister of Labour was made responsible to Parliament for the administration of both schemes, although an independent Unemployment Assistance Board was set up to operate the Unemployment Assistance Scheme.

From the onset of heavy unemployment in the early 1920's almost throughout the inter-war years, the machinery of the Employment Exchanges was required very largely for the registration of claims for unemployment benefit and its payment. At many exchanges throughout the country tens of thousands of unemployed workers attended twice a week to prove that they were unemployed and were 'genuinely seeking work', as well as coming to draw their unemployment pay on a third day. This was an overwhelming burden on the exchanges, but the experience they underwent was a valuable preparation for the handling of later tasks in which large numbers of persons were involved.

During these inter-war years the Employment Exchanges endeavoured to carry on their original functions in connection with employment and the placing of workers and the development of the youth employment service. But it was natural that these functions should be overshadowed by unemployment insurance and the result was that the Ministry became primarily associated in the minds of the public with the relief of unemployment and distress.

Industrial Relations between the Wars

The other main preoccupation of the Ministry during these years was that of industrial relations. The Government had become so concerned about industrial relations during the war that they had set up a Committee on the relations between Employers and Employed under the chairmanship of the Speaker of the House of Commons, Mr J. H. Whitley. As a result of the Committee's Report Joint Industrial Councils were established in a substantial number of industries, and a large number of works committees in individual firms were set up. At the same time a permanent court of arbitration, the Industrial Court, was established under the Industrial Courts Act, 1919, which also gave power to hold inquiries into trade disputes for the purpose of informing Parliament and the public of the facts. In addition, the power to set up Trade Boards was extended by the Trade Boards Act, 1918, to cover badly organised trades. These measures proved in due course to be of considerable effect in improving labour-management relations and providing effective conciliation machinery but the early part of the 1920's was a period of great industrial unrest. There were many bitter disputes and long stoppages of work such, for example, as the engineering disputes about managerial functions and the prolonged stoppage in the coalmining industry. This unrest culminated in the general strike of 1926.

The Ministry's powers of intervention in trade disputes, which had been extended by the Industrial Courts Act, were used with circumspection. The Department did not normally take action in connection with a trade dispute unless invited to do so by one or other of the parties and, in any case, did not intervene unless and until the means for settling the dispute through the agreed arrangements in an industry had been exhausted. Courts of Inquiry were used with considerable success, the first one set up in 1920 being in connection with the threatened national stoppage of work in the docks. It was at this inquiry that Mr Ernest Bevin acquired the name of the 'Dockers' K.C.' Other inquiries included those into disputes in the engineering and building industries and in the railway shops.

This period of industrial unrest tested the resources of the Ministry and at the same time provided it with much experience in the handling of disputes. It was the policy of the Department, a policy consistently followed under successive Governments, to encourage industries to set up their own voluntary negotiating arrangements and to settle their own disputes. This policy suffered a set-back as a result of the general strike. There were casualties among the Joint Industrial Councils set up after the Whitley Report, only 47 of the 106 that came into existence from 1918 to the end of 1921 surviving. However, the idea of Whitleyism gradually re-established itself and, as organisation on both sides improved, a better relationship began to manifest itself. As a result there was a growth of joint voluntary negotiating machinery in many industries and the establishment of agreed arrangements providing for the settlement of disputes. This brought about a marked improvement in the relations between employers and workpeople and in the 1930's there was a very considerable reduction in the number of days lost through stoppages caused by trade disputes. This, however, did not mean that there was any material lessening of the volume of conciliation work the Ministry was called upon to do. By this time the good offices of the Department had become more acceptable to employers and unions and the help and advice of the conciliation officers of the Department were sought with increasing frequency and many incipient disputes were prevented from reaching the stage of a stoppage of work.

While the relief of unemployment and the handling of industrial relations were necessarily the main duties of the Department during the inter-war years and overshadowed its other activities, no great change, apart from that of dealing with international labour problems, took place in its basic functions—it was a question of events altering the emphasis of these functions. So far as was practicable, therefore, it continued to carry out its functions relating to the placing of workers in employment, to youth employment, to the disabled and to schemes of training for the unemployed.

International Labour

It was recognised at the end of the 1914–18 war that labour standards throughout the world were of concern to all countries, both from the competitive aspect and from that of social justice. Accordingly, in 1919, the International Labour Organisation was established under the Treaty of Versailles for the purpose, as stated in the Constitution of the Organisation, of securing the permanent peace of the world by the establishment of social justice through an improvement of conditions of labour.

The general responsibility for all government business concerned with the Organisation was centred in the Ministry of Labour. The unique feature of the Organisation was, and still is, its tripartite character, being representative of Governments, employers and workers. In order to carry out the aim of promoting social justice throughout the world, it has formulated international labour standards by means of Conventions or Recommendations adopted by the General Conference of the Organisation. In this work the Department has taken its full part at all times.

(3) THE WAR OF 1939–45

Following the Munich crisis of September, 1938, the shadow of coming events was becoming discernible and all Government Departments were required to make preparations for the possibility of war. These preparations, so far as they affected the Ministry, were chiefly directed towards the mobilisation of the manpower of the country and its fair distribution as between the Armed Forces and industry. In order to carry out these aims some important extensions of the functions of the Ministry took place.

National Service Campaign

In the first place, the Department was required in January, 1939, to assist in the carrying through of a campaign with a view to persuading men and women to volunteer at the Employment Exchanges for service with the Armed Forces, the Civil Defence Services, or any specialised civilian work. Then, in the following May, the Military Training Act, 1939, came into operation under which young men were required on reaching the age of 20 years to undergo six months' military training in the Armed Forces. Before this Act was passed a decision of the greatest importance to the Department was taken by the Government. It was decided that the administration of the Act should be entrusted to the Ministry. This was an historic decision, entrusting to a civil Department for the first time in the nation's history the call-up of men to the Forces. It was also the occasion of the first great widening of the Ministry's functions and led to the Department becoming later in the year the Ministry of Labour and National Service and as such responsible during the Second World War for the mobilisation of the whole manpower of the country.

Mobilisation of Manpower

The National Service (Armed Forces) Act, 1939, was passed through all its stages in both Houses of Parliament and came into operation on the day on which Britain declared war—3rd September, 1939. This Act superseded the Military Training Act and imposed liability for military service on all male British subjects in Great Britain aged 19–40 inclusive. Under it, additional duties and responsibilities were imposed on the Ministry ranging from the initial stage of registration by age-groups at the Employment Exchanges to medical examination, postponement of service on hardship grounds, deferment of service on account of the importance of certain occupations, reference to Tribunals of claims on conscientious grounds, and finally to the posting of men to the Armed Forces.

Amending legislation in the course of 1941 made provision for calling up men for Civil Defence, extended the upper age limit of liability for service to 51, and imposed liability for service upon women.

This granting of the power to call up women for the Armed Forces compulsorily was another historic step. Never before had women in Great Britain been conscripted and the Department was called upon to exercise functions of a nature which, if not handled with great care, could have aroused deep feelings. The Minister, Mr Ernest Bevin, decided to give women the option of being called up for the Women's Forces or of being directed into war work. Those who did not express any preference were sent to the Forces or to industry according to the current requirements and this flexible system was a great success.

On the civilian side, the Minister was given powers by Orders made under the Emergency Powers (Defence) Act of 24th August, 1939, to mobilise and control civilian labour. These powers were drastically widened and strengthened in May, 1940, by Regulation 58A made under the Emergency Powers (Defence) Act, 1940. This regulation gave authority to register workers, to regulate their engagement by employers and to 'direct any person, of any age, in Great Britain to perform any service in the United Kingdom which that person was capable of performing, at the "rate for the job"'.

The Ministry was thus given comprehensive powers to deal with manpower as a whole and in all its aspects, whether for military requirements or for civilian purposes. The two main tasks in mobilising manpower were, first, to ensure an optimum and fair distribution between the Armed Forces, Civil Defence and civilian war industries and services, and second, to secure a proper division between competing civilian needs. The most efficient use of manpower, especially of the skilled and technical manpower, was a third important task.

To carry out the first two tasks, what may be called a 'master plan' was devised. This was the manpower budget which introduced a system of allocation of manpower to which Departments were required to work. The manpower budget was prepared by means of estimates of the manpower expected to become available during a given future period, together with estimates of requirements prepared by the Service Departments, the War Supply Departments and the Departments responsible for the various civilian needs of the country. Needless to say, the requirements always outstripped the numbers available. Broad lines of allocation were determined periodically by the War Cabinet. These allocations were translated into practical effect so far as men were concerned by means of a system of reserved occupations under which men above a specified age in listed occupations of great importance to war industries and essential civilian services would not be called up. This system was subsequently gradually superseded by one of individual deferment of call-up in certain occupations—a more refined instrument than that of block reservation. As has already been stated, women in the limited number of age-classes who were called up had the option of serving in the Forces or in industry. These methods determined the main allocation of manpower as between the Forces and industry.

From 1940 up to the middle of 1945, in pursuance of the general plan, men and women were registered by the Employment Exchanges in successive age-groups or in specified occupations for transfer to work of national importance if not so employed, the power of direction being used as necessary. The distribution of the manpower thus made available was effected, in co-operation with the Supply Department, by a system of labour preferences in accordance with the competing needs of war industries and services and civilian needs.

An indication of the vast and successful operations of the Employment Exchanges is given by the following figures. When the peak of manpower mobilisation was reached in September, 1943, nearly 15 million of the 15,920,000 men of working age in Great Britain were in the Forces, Civil Defence or in industry, commerce and the professions; the balance were mainly men otherwise unfit for employment, invalids or students. Of approximately 16,020,000 women of working age, about 7,250,000 were in the Forces, Civil Defence or in industry, commerce and the professions; these included about 90 per cent of the single women aged 18–40 and about 80 per cent of the married women and widows in the same age-groups with no young children.

Efficient Use of Manpower

The third main task of securing the full and most efficient use of manpower in order to obtain the optimum production in industry involved the Department in a number of different measures and in the use of further powers.

While the economical use of labour depended mainly on the energy and initiative of employers, the Ministry found it necessary to appoint labour supply inspectors with technical knowledge and experience to help in the breaking down of highly skilled work into less skilled operations. They also made a critical examination of employers' demands for labour and advised on manpower economies to ensure that the available supply of scarce skilled labour was used to the best advantage.

It was clear at an early stage of mobilisation that the supply of skilled men and of technicians and scientists would have to be greatly increased. In addition to dealing with this problem of skill by means of dilution, Government Training Centres were greatly expanded and large numbers of men trained to a relatively high degree of skill. Subsequently these centres were extended to train women and were supplemented by the provision of places in technical and commercial schools and at selected industrial establishments.

Steps were taken through the Technical and Scientific Register which had been set up within the Ministry shortly before the war and through the Appointments Offices established in 1942 within the existing organisation of the Ministry to conserve technical, scientific, professional and higher administrative manpower. Similarly, measures were taken to meet the growing shortage of nurses and midwives, service in these professions being regarded as alternative to service in the Women's Auxiliary Services.[1]

The need to use the productive capacity of everyone in the nation led to the introduction in 1941 of a scheme for the training and resettlement of the disabled. The scheme provided both for those who had been disabled during their Forces service and for those who had been disabled in other ways and at other times. An inter-Departmental Committee was set up later in the same year under the chairmanship of Mr George Tomlinson, then Parliamentary Secretary to the Ministry, and this Committee, which reported in January, 1943, recommended that special facilities for the rehabilitation and resettlement of the disabled should be embodied in permanent legislation. The Disabled Persons (Employment) Act, 1944, implemented the Committee's recommendations on training, industrial rehabilitation and employment, while the recommendations on medical rehabilitation were taken into account in shaping the National Health Service.

By Restriction on Engagement Orders under which employers were required to obtain their labour (men and women) through the Employment Exchanges, the 'poaching' by employers of skilled labour through the inducement of bonuses and higher wages was largely stopped and the manpower in agriculture and mining conserved. Similarly, by the Essential Work Order unnecessary turnover of labour was prevented. In specified undertakings, designated by the Minister as essential to the life of the community, an employer could not dismiss a worker, except for serious misconduct, without the permission of the National Service Officer (an officer of the Department designated under the Order for the purpose), and a worker was similarly debarred from leaving his employment. Workers had to be regular in attendance and to work the prescribed hours; in return they were given a guaranteed weekly wage and could rely on satisfactory arrangements for their safety, health and welfare.

Safety, Health and Welfare

These safety, health and welfare arrangements for assisting to maintain the efficient use of manpower were made possible by the transfer in June, 1940, of the administration of the Factories Acts from the Home Office to the Ministry—an extremely important development in the functions of the Department. With the exercising of increasing control over the movement of individual workers, particularly women, the Minister, Mr Ernest Bevin, felt the need to ensure that the task of maintaining the necessary standards of

[1] For subsequent developments, see pages 52 and 53.

working conditions inside the factories was fully co-ordinated with manpower policy. Powers were given to the Chief Inspector of Factories to direct employers engaged on munitions or on government contracts to make satisfactory arrangements for their workers by the provision of medical supervision, nursing and first-aid services, welfare services, and canteens where hot meals could be purchased. A factory canteen advisory service was set up to advise employers within the sphere of the Factories Acts on the establishment, organisation and management of canteen and other food services for employees. Subsequent Orders provided for the welfare of workers on building and civil engineering sites and in dockyards.

As a supplement to the transfer of the administration of the Factories Acts to the Ministry of Labour, the Minister developed an organisation for dealing with the welfare of workers outside the factories—such as the provision of reception hostels and of lodgings for transferred workers, and special transport arrangements. The Minister also established the National Service Hostels Corporation in 1941 to set up and manage hostels for transferred workers living away from home and special provision was made by way of hostels and other welfare arrangements for merchant sailors while in port.

The measures so far referred to in connection with making the most efficient use of manpower with a view to securing maximum production have related mainly to the supply and control of labour. There were, however, other measures that were taken in the field of industrial relations, measures of very great importance and effect.

Industrial Relations

Reference has already been made to the National Joint Advisory Council. This was set up in October, 1939, by the Minister (Mr Ernest Brown) to advise him on all matters affecting industry in which employers and workers had a common interest. The Council was composed of representatives of the British Employers' Confederation and of the Trades Union Congress, and it met under the Minister's chairmanship. When Mr Bevin became Minister in May, 1940, he formed an executive committee of the Council, called the Joint Consultative Committee. This Committee sat regularly throughout the war under Mr Bevin's chairmanship. All important matters of manpower and industrial relations policy were put to this Committee for their advice. On no occasion was there disagreement on this Committee on any major issue of policy and the carrying with him of the organised employers and workers of the country was an important factor in enabling the Minister to develop his plans for mobilising the nation and put them into effect with such success.

One outstanding measure that was put into operation following advice from the Joint Consultative Committee was the Conditions of Employment and National Arbitration Order, 1940, generally known as 'Order 1305'. This prohibited lock-outs and strikes in connection with any trade dispute unless the dispute had been reported to the Minister in accordance with the Order and he had failed to refer it for arbitration within three weeks to a National Arbitration Tribunal established under the Order for this purpose. The award of the Tribunal was to be legally binding. The Order did not render industry immune from stoppages, nor did it diminish the powers of the Minister to seek the settlement of a dispute in any of the ways already open to him, but it did help to create an atmosphere unfavourable to any serious dislocation of the war effort through such conflicts.

Another important agreement made between employers and trade unions following discussions on the Joint Consultative Committee provided for the temporary relaxation of existing industrial customs in order to permit the breakdown of skilled jobs and the introduction into industry of large numbers of unskilled and semi-skilled workers, many of whom were women.

It has been necessary to refer in some detail to the powers conferred on the Ministry and the measures taken by it during the war, as it was during this period that its functions were so greatly expanded. Owing to its scarcity, manpower became a vital factor—perhaps the most vital factor—in the planning of the war effort and accounted for the important part that the Department played during the war years, when its work pointed the way to the kind of Department that should emerge to play a constructive part in the industrial and social life of the country in peace-time.

(4) POST-WAR DEMOBILISATION AND RESETTLEMENT

The immediate tasks when the war ended were demobilisation and resettlement—demobilisation of the Armed Forces and industrial demobilisation. During the war the most careful and prolonged consideration was given to the plans for demobilisation and resettlement and in co-operation with the other Departments concerned these were worked out in detail by the Department. It was necessary that these plans should be fair and should be seen to be fair, and should work smoothly and with speed. Here again the machinery of the Employment Exchanges was a great asset and enabled large numbers of men and women to be dealt with quickly, fairly and in a spirit of helpfulness.

Military Demobilisation

Demobilisation of the men and women in the Forces, which began on 18th June, 1945, was governed by what was commonly known as 'the Bevin Scheme'. Under this scheme, releases from the Forces were based either on age and length of service (Class A) or on account of special qualifications for urgent work of national importance (Class B). It was recognised that the combination of age and length of service was the fairest method as between one individual and another. This, however, did not wholly serve the national interest and it was decided that there should be a limited number of releases out of turn. An essential factor of this out of turn release was its limited nature. It was necessary in the interests of fairness to maintain so far as possible the criterion of age and length of service and accordingly out of turn releases were not permitted to exceed 10 per cent of the general releases. These out of turn releases were planned most carefully to meet the requirements of urgent work of national importance, about half of them being for building or civil engineering. Men and women in the Forces were fully informed about the demobilisation scheme and how it would work and were at the same time told about the arrangements for resettlement that had been made for their benefit. This enabled them to plan ahead for their future. By the end of 1947 nearly 5 million men and women had been released and absorbed into industry, commerce and the professions without serious unemployment occurring.

On demobilisation large numbers of men and women needed advice on a diversity of matters connected with resettlement and the Ministry set up Resettlement Advice Offices throughout the country to supplement the general service given by the Employment Exchanges. This advice service was obviously of a temporary nature, but for the time being it brought the Department into many new fields.

During this period the main function of the Employment Exchanges was to find suitable work for men and women coming out of the Forces, but at the same time they helped to carry out a number of special schemes. Under the Reinstatement in Civil Employment Act, 1944, men and women called up to the Forces had the right to reinstatement in their pre-enlistment employment, if reasonable and practical, while, through the Interrupted Apprenticeship Scheme, special arrangements were made for those whose apprenticeship had been interrupted by military service. The Appointments Service of the Ministry, in conjunction with the Departments of Education and Agriculture, operated a Further Education and Training Scheme and a Business Training Scheme to help those whose education and training for the higher ranks of industry, commerce and the professions had been interrupted by the war. For men who had been running small businesses on their own account before the war a Resettlement Grants Scheme was put into operation; the scheme also applied to those who were disabled in the war and wished to enter business on their own account for the first time. In addition, vocational training facilities were expanded and large numbers with no industrial experience before serving in the Forces were given training in industry or in the Government Training Centres.

Industrial Demobilisation

While military demobilisation was going on, industrial demobilisation proceeded rapidly. Many firms changed directly from war work to civilian work, but at the same time there was very considerable displacement of labour, especially from 'shadow' factories and temporary war-time extensions of factories. The resettlement in other employment of civilian war workers therefore needed arrangements analogous to some of those devised for men and women released from the Forces. A scheme for release from civilian employment, based on a system of priorities, which had been worked out during the war, was put into operation immediately the war ended. Under this scheme men over 65, women over 60 and women with household responsibilities or those who wished to join their husbands on release from the Forces were free to leave their war jobs when the war in Europe ended. Those in these categories who wished to transfer to work nearer home, and those who had worked away from home for three years or more were given priority in transfer to other work of importance offering prospects of permanency unless there were strong production reasons to the contrary. Where redundancy existed in establishments after these classes had been released the scheme laid down an order of discharge covering young men to be called up to the Forces, those urgently needed in other work, those who had worked away from home for more than one and less than three years, and those whose release was in accordance with the various industrial agreements.

The demobilisation of men and women from the Forces was finished by the end of 1947, and the reallocation of industrial manpower was completed by the early months of 1948. All this was a considerable achievement, particularly as at no time was there any substantial increase in unemployment during this vast change-over of manpower.

Following the end of the war, the various labour controls were progressively withdrawn or relaxed, with the exception of the Order under which employers were required to obtain their labour through the Employment Exchanges. This was subsequently with-drawn in 1951 but when the Defence programme made large demands on manpower in 1952 it was reimposed in a slightly different form in order to assist the exchanges in placing men and women in vacancies of importance to the national effort. It was revoked in 1956.

(5) POST-WAR DEVELOPMENTS

After the period of demobilisation and resettlement and the with-drawal of the war-time controls of labour, the Ministry's activities centred to an increasing extent on its normal peace-time function of the placing and distribution of manpower. In the years immediately after the war there was a high demand particularly for skilled labour and for some kinds of semi-skilled and unskilled labour. Firms producing goods for export and those endeavouring to meet the pent-up or increasing demands of the home market for consumer goods needed large increases of manpower, and the manufacturing and constructional industries clamoured for tools, materials and labour. The supply of manpower was inadequate to meet all the demands upon it and the country experienced a period of full, or over-full employment. When the gap in the supply of consumer goods had been filled the manpower position eased to some extent, but there was still a shortage of labour in some areas and in some occupations, and a shortage of young persons and of skilled men, with a growing scarcity of scientists and technicians. Moreover, with the expansion of the Defence programme after 1951 and the increasing requirements for the export trade, the general scarcity of manpower once again became more pronounced.

Maintenance of Full Employment

It was the aim of the Government, as stated in the White Paper on Employment Policy,[1] to maintain a high and stable level of employ-ment. In this the Government was greatly helped by demands for manpower for manufacturing and constructional industries at home, expanding export industries and the Defence programme. But to maintain employment at the highest level the planning of investment and production and the organisation of the labour market were necessary, as well as a balanced development of industry in the 'Special Areas'—the areas which had been specially vulnerable to unemployment in the past. In all this the Department had an important part to play. First of all, full and up-to-date information on employment and unemployment was needed in order to enable the Government to measure the present state and future prospects

[1] Cmd. 6527 of May, 1944.

D

of the various industries of the country together with information about manpower trends, areas of labour surplus and shortage, and the extent of short-time and overtime working. This information was obtained by means of monthly reports from the Employment Exchanges to the regional offices of the Department, supplemented by monthly returns from employers.

Supply, Distribution and Efficient Use of Manpower

The other duties which fell to the Ministry in connection with maintaining full employment were to endeavour to increase the supply of manpower and to secure its more efficient use by improving its quality and securing its most advantageous distribution.

Reference has already been made in Chapter I to some of the special measures taken to augment the supply of manpower and at the same time to assist particular classes of the community where special difficulties exist. Reference to seven such types of case will have to suffice—the employment of foreign workers, the employment of older workers, the reabsorption of ex-regular members of the Forces, the industrial rehabilitation, training and employment of disabled persons, the recruitment and distribution of nurses and midwives, the supply of technical and scientific workers, and the employment of young persons.

Employment of Foreign Workers

After the war the Ministry sponsored schemes under which large numbers of foreign workers were recruited. By the end of 1949, these foreign workers, together with ex-members of the Polish Armed Forces under British Command and their civilian dependants, had added about a quarter of a million to the working population of the country. Since 1951, nearly 16,000 Italian men and women have been recruited for industries such as textiles, coalmining, iron ore mining, steel founding, tinplate and brickmaking. The selection of foreign workers, arrangements for their transport, their training and placing in employment, involved a considerable amount of work and often produced a number of difficult problems for the Department.

Employment of Older Workers

Finding employment for the older worker and his continued employment after reaching the age of normal retirement assumed importance in view of the general shortage of manpower, while at the same time being part of a general social and economic problem arising from the increasing proportion of older people in the population. In 1952, a National Advisory Committee was appointed to advise and assist the Minister in promoting the employment of older people. This Committee recommended that the test for engagement should be capacity not age, and that all employed men and women who could give effective service should be given the opportunity to continue at work if they so wished. Following these recommendations some improvement has taken place in the employment prospects of the older worker and many employers have revised their engagement and retirement practices.

Resettlement of ex-Regulars

As was mentioned in Chapter I, an Advisory Council to assist the Department and the Ministry of Defence was established in 1950 on 'The Relationship between Employment in the Services and Civilian Life' with the Permanent Secretary of the Ministry of Labour and National Service in the Chair. The help of the Council, which consisted of representatives of the three Service Departments, the Ministries of Defence, Education and Labour, and of educational authorities, employers and trade unions, was sought on the best means of securing an integration of Service and civilian life in order to provide the opportunity of a continuous career through the Services and industry. With the approval of the Council, the Ministry obtained the agreement of many employers to fill a proportion of their new labour requirements by the recruitment of ex-Regulars, or to relax age limits in their favour; in some cases preference was given to ex-Regulars for certain kinds of jobs or for training at the firm's expense. Also, following discussions between the Service Departments and the trade unions, training given in most Service trades was recognised for the purposes of trade union membership. In addition, the Department established vocational and business training schemes to give special help to those whose Service experience has no civilian equivalent. These measures proved of considerable assistance to ex-Regulars in resettling themselves in civilian life on leaving the Forces.

The Industrial Rehabilitation, Training and Employment of Disabled Persons

Another source of manpower that was made use of to an increasing extent after the end of the war was the disabled. Brief reference has already been made to the scheme for the training and settlement in employment of disabled persons established during the war—a scheme which will always be associated with the then Parliamentary Secretary to the Ministry, Mr George Tomlinson. The objects of this scheme were essentially humanitarian, but its immediate purposes were to assist the war effort by making the most effective

use of the services that disabled persons could give and to provide
for the rehabilitation of war casualties. Following the passing of the
Disabled Persons (Employment) Act, 1944, a permanent scheme was
established, providing for the industrial rehabilitation, training and
employment of disabled persons. The main features of this have been
described already.

In 1953 it was decided that a new Committee of Inquiry should
be set up under the chairmanship of Lord Piercy to review the
whole field of services for the disabled. The Committee reported in
1956 and, although it made a number of detailed recommendations
on resettlement facilities, it found that the framework of the Disabled Persons (Employment) Act needed little alteration in the light
of the practical experience gained since its enactment.

The Recruitment and Distribution of Nurses and Midwives

Brief reference has already been made to the growing shortage
during the war of nurses and midwives. When, in the middle of the
war, the Ministry of Health asked the Ministry to tackle the recruitment and distribution of nurses and midwives, the position was
approaching one of crisis and there was a danger of a number of
hospitals having to close some of their wards for lack of staff. The
nursing and midwifery field was something new for the Department.
That being so, its immediate reaction was to consult the nursing and
midwifery organisations on the one hand and the hospital authorities
on the other and to seek their advice on the problems involved.
From this emerged the National Advisory Council on Recruitment
of Nurses and Midwives, established in 1942 to advise the Minister,
who was the Chairman of the Council, on all matters connected
with the recruitment and distribution of nurses and midwives. This
was a singularly successful example of co-operation between the
Department and the organisations concerned. Many matters
affecting the recruitment and training of nurses and midwives were
dealt with by the Council and, as indicated below, resulted in a
substantial improvement in the supply.

The Department established in 1943 a Nursing Appointments
Service. This originally functioned through 31 separate offices, to
each of which a qualified nurse was attached as technical nursing
officer. At the end of 1957 there were 165 such offices, mainly housed
in the women's department of Employment Exchanges, with 21
technical nursing officers—about half of them stationed in the
Regional Offices; these nursing officers provide help and advice for
the nursing offices and the exchanges on technical matters. Besides
giving advice on entry to the professions of nursing, midwifery and

auxiliary medical services, the Nursing Appointments Service provides advisory and employment placing facilities for those already in these professions. While there is still a shortage of nurses, particularly for mental hospitals, the general improvement in the position can be judged from the following figures:

From the time in 1942 when the Department took over the recruitment of nurses and midwives to the end of 1955, the total number of nurses and midwives increased by over 40 per cent; in the period 1948 to 1955 the increase was about 20 per cent. So far as trained nurses are concerned, there was an increase from the end of 1948 to the end of 1955 of about 28 per cent in the numbers of full-time trained nurses and of about 35 per cent in the numbers of full- and part-time trained nurses. And it must be remembered that this great gain was achieved at a time of serious shortage of manpower.

More recently modifications have been made in the arrangements for dealing with nurses and midwives and, while the Nursing Appointments Offices continue to operate, the Advisory Council no longer exists.

The Supply of Technical and Scientific Workers

The Technical and Scientific Register for highly qualified engineers and scientists has been maintained since the end of the war in view of the continuing demand for all those persons with technical qualifications. A special Unit has been established to deal with the recruitment of highly qualified experts for under-developed countries under such schemes as the Colombo Plan and the United Nations Technical Assistance Scheme. The Register continues to be guided by the Technical Personnel Committee.

The Appointments Offices were closed, for reasons of economy, in March, 1957, and the work of placing persons of professional, managerial and executive status was transferred to 48 specially selected Employment Exchanges, at which arrangements were made to hold a Professional and Executive Register.

Youth Employment

Owing to the fall in the birth-rate in the late 1920's and the early 1930's there was a grave and growing scarcity of young persons after the war, a scarcity which emphasised the need to ensure that new entrants to employment are given the opportunity of obtaining suitable and satisfactory work, and are adequately trained and properly used.

A state Youth Employment Service designed to advise boys and girls leaving school on their choice of career, to assist them to find a suitable job, and to be available for further advice if required, has been in operation since before the First World War. Central responsibility for this service has lain with the Ministry since 1927, but local responsibility was divided between the Ministry of Labour on the one hand and the local education authorities on the other.

In 1948 important developments in the service took place as a result of the recommendations of a Committee of representatives of employers, trade unions, local education authorities, the Ministry of Education, the Scottish Education Department, and the Ministry of Labour. The Committee's Report, commonly known as the Ince Report, set out the principles on which a youth employment service should be based and was widely accepted. Most of its recommendations were put into operation, those needing legislative sanction being embodied in the Employment and Training Act, 1948.

As a result of the Committee's recommendations the scope of the service was widened, but its three main functions continued to be the provision of vocational guidance for boys and girls about to leave school, their placing in suitable employment and their subsequent after-care.

A Central Youth Employment Executive, responsible to the Minister of Labour but including in its membership not only a Chairman and two other members of the Ministry of Labour staff, but also an official from each of the two Education Departments, was established as a central administration to run the service. Locally the dual system continued but it was stabilised by giving the education authorities, including those in Scotland, a once-for-all option, which many of them exercised, of providing the service in their areas. A National Youth Employment Council, with separate Advisory Committees for Scotland and Wales, was established to advise the Minister. Locally, the system of Youth Employment Committees was continued.

In recent years the service has been developed and has become more effective and more widely used as the knowledge and experience of youth employment officers have increased.

The Efficient Use of Manpower

The more efficient use of manpower through an improvement in its quality and its better distribution involved the provision of training facilities to train both new entrants and existing labour and to fit workers from declining industries for jobs in expanding industries. In this the training provided by industry was assisted by that done by the Government Training Centres run by the Department. Assistance was also given to industry in training its supervisory management to cope with the problems of training new personnel, handling relations with workers and introducing new methods through the scheme of Training Within Industry for Supervisors (T.W.I.) introduced by the Ministry towards the end of the war. The question of supervisory training in all its aspects was studied by a Committee of experts drawn from industry and education under the Ministry's chairmanship and the Committee's Report published in 1954 formed a useful basis for discussion and development within industry; the T.W.I. Scheme has been revised and brought up to date and a fourth training programme dealing with works safety has been introduced.

Another factor affecting the efficiency of manpower was its mobility, the increase of which was assisted by the removal of obstacles to the transfer of workers from one area to another (which may involve in some cases transfer to a different occupation), by means of financial assistance and by training. A further means to the same end was the giving of advice to other Government Departments as to the areas of comparatively good labour supply to which new or expanding industries might be persuaded to go.

Industrial Relations

One of the main tasks facing the Ministry after the war was the promotion and maintenance of industrial peace. Order 1305, introduced in 1940, making strikes and lock-outs illegal and providing for compulsory arbitration, was revoked in 1951 and replaced by another Industrial Disputes Order, which withdrew the prohibition on strikes and lock-outs but retained the system of arbitration at the instance of only one party as far as disputes on wages and conditions of employment were concerned. At the same time, in order to encourage and strengthen voluntary negotiating machinery, the right to invoke the Order was restricted to the parties to such machinery where it existed. Where no such machinery existed, the use of the Order, apart from individual employers, was restricted to those organisations or trade unions which represented a substantial proportion of employers or workers in the industry or section of the industry concerned. This Order is still in operation.[1]

Compared with the period of grave industrial unrest after the First World War the years after the Second World War were years of comparative industrial peace, although some large and serious strikes have taken place. These, however, must be not allowed to obscure the very real progress which has been made. The Ministry continued to build up its expert conciliation services and by patient and persistent effort succeeded in securing some extension of voluntary negotiating machinery and of joint arrangements for settling disputes.

[1] This Order was revoked in December, 1958.

Safety, Health and Welfare

The transfer of the Factory Department from the Home Office was made permanent in March, 1946, and represented an important and logical addition to the functions of the Ministry. As Mr Bevin said when speaking of the transfer of powers in the House of Commons in July, 1952: 'The transfer gave to the Ministry of Labour, in its development of the other schemes associated with the mobilisation of manpower, valuable experience, long tradition, great knowledge of the factories of the country and contacts which serve a double purpose.' Some idea of the extension of the functions of the Department by this transfer can be gauged by the fact that factory legislation constitutes a comprehensive code covering safety at work, the prevention of industrial disease, the hours of employment of women and young persons, and the health and welfare measures which cover cleanliness, overcrowding, ventilation, heating, lighting, rest facilities, and the provision of first aid. All these matters have repercussions on both labour supply and industrial relations.

Since the war there has been a continuing improvement in the standards of safety, health and welfare both by the application of the Factories Acts through the Factory Inspectorate and as a result of the voluntary efforts and co-operation of employers and workers and their organisations. Also, the Department has kept abreast of many new developments in industry, such as the use of radio-active materials, and has ensured that management and workers alike have been made aware of the new health hazards and the necessity to take measures to counter them. Although considerable progress was being made in combating these hazards through advances in both medical and technological knowledge, it was felt that more comprehensive measures of health protection were necessary in the light of growing needs. Accordingly, in 1954, following discussions with medical and industrial organisations, the Minister decided to take steps to stimulate the further development of industrial health services in workplaces covered by the Factories Acts, including the provision of good environmental conditions at the place of work, of protection against industrial disease and poisoning, and of adequate medical and nursing supervision and first-aid. To assist him in this development he reconstituted the Industrial Health Advisory Committee.

International Labour

The work of the Overseas Department of the Ministry has increased substantially since the end of the war owing to the growth in scope and importance of the activities of the International Labour Organisation, the establishment of a number of other international organisations, the development of the Labour Attaché service, and the increased numbers of foreign workers coming to this country mainly as a result of the war in Europe.

International Labour Organisation

The International Labour Organisation is the only body set up under the Treaty of Versailles that survived the Second World War. Since 1946 it has been associated with the United Nations as one of the 'Specialised Agencies'. In addition to expanding its work of formulating international labour standards by means of Conventions or Recommendations, the Organisation has greatly increased its operational activities by participating in the Expanded Technical Assistance Programme of the United Nations and by assisting Member States with advice on labour legislation and by other action on various labour matters. These increased activities have reacted on the work of the Ministry as the normal channel of communication between the Organisation and the United Kingdom Government, work involving frequent consultation with other branches in the Ministry and with other Government Departments.

Other International Organisations

A number of other international organisations such as the Economic and Social Council of the United Nations, and the various Specialised Agencies such as the United Nations Educational, Scientific and Cultural Organisation, the World Health Organisation and the Food and Agriculture Organisation, as well as regional organisations such as the Organisation for European Economic Co-operation, Western European Union, the Council of Europe, and the North Atlantic Treaty Organisation, frequently deal with problems of concern to the Ministry either because of its domestic responsibilities or because of its responsibilities for United Kingdom relations with the International Labour Organisation. It has been necessary, therefore, for the Ministry to keep itself informed of the activities of these organisations and in some cases to participate in them.

Labour Attachés

A development of much importance took place after the war following an experiment started in 1942. In that year, the first appointment of a Labour Attaché was made to the British Embassy at Washington giving effect to an idea conceived by Mr Ernest Bevin and agreed by the Foreign Secretary. It was thought that, with the growing political influence of organised labour and the increasing importance of labour and social questions in national and international affairs, an attaché specialising in these matters could give valuable assistance in the work of a Diplomatic Mission abroad by maintaining close contact with the appropriate Government Departments, associations of employers and workers, and organisations and institutions operating in the labour and industrial fields.

From this beginning the Labour Attaché service has been developed until there are now Labour Attachés at Diplomatic Missions in many parts of the world, including Europe, Asia, the Middle East and North, Central and South America.

Migration of Labour and Employment of Aliens

Under provisions which have been in operation for nearly 40 years, and in their latest form are contained in the Aliens Order, 1953, the Ministry has the responsibility of dealing with applications from foreigners for permission to take employment in this country. The numbers of foreigners coming here greatly increased after the war, mainly because of large numbers of European volunteer workers from displaced persons camps in Germany and because of the resettlement of Poles who fought with the Allied Armies during the war. Also, in order to mitigate the grave shortage of workers in certain industries, foreign workers, mainly Italian, were brought to this country for employment. Opportunities of employment for foreign workers have more recently diminished.

The Ministry has also been called upon to an increasing extent to assist Commonwealth Governments who have been seeking to increase the numbers of immigrants from this country both generally and in particular occupations.

PART II

Manpower

CHAPTER III

Employment Policy and the General Employment Service

*

THE Ministry is the Government Department primarily concerned with employment and the use of manpower. It is responsible for collecting information about the supply of and demand for labour, both short- and long-term, for drawing attention to shortages of labour and to surpluses with their attendant unemployment, for encouraging the most efficient distribution and use of labour in the national interest, and for providing an employment service which facilitates the attainment of this objective.

The Ministry derives its powers to administer a general employment service in the main from the Employment and Training Act, 1948. The basis for its functions in the sphere of employment policy is not contained in legislation, although certain of the functions are laid down in the White Paper on Employment Policy presented to Parliament in 1944.[1]

This dealt with both the short-term problems which would be met in the period of transition from war to peace and the long-term problems likely to be encountered in the maintenance of full employment. It made clear the limitations of government action, and stressed that while government policy would be directed to bringing about conditions favourable to a high and stable level of employment, employment could not be created by government action alone. The success of any such policy must depend ultimately on the support of the community as a whole and especially on the efforts of employers and workers in industry; without a rising standard of industrial efficiency a high level of employment cannot be combined with a rising standard of living. The main items of the policy outlined as necessary to promote circumstances favourable to full employment dealt with the maintenance of total expenditure, the stability of prices and wages, the balanced distribution of industry and labour and the mobility of labour. The Ministry is chiefly concerned with the last two of these four items.

[1] Employment Policy (Cmd. 6527), 16th May, 1944. H.M. Stationery Office, price 6d.

Responsibility for the Ministry's employment functions at its headquarters rests with the Employment Department. This Department deals with general employment policy; information relating to the employment situation nationally and locally; advice on employment aspects of economic policy and of distribution of industry policy; policy matters in connection with the employment of older workers; the employment service as administered through Employment Exchanges, the Technical and Scientific Register; policy and co-ordination of arrangements for placing foreign workers in employment.

General Employment Situation

In the post-war period the Ministry has had to meet the continuing problem of the general shortage of labour, resulting from industrial expansion. This has been met in part by the recruitment of married women and part-time and retired workers, and the Ministry has taken an active part in developing this source of supply. At the same time the shortage has made easier the Ministry's task of giving special assistance to the disabled, older workers and ex-regular Servicemen and women. The Ministry has taken special measures to improve the employment prospects of both older workers and ex-regular Servicemen, with the object of assisting members of these classes and increasing the supply of labour. An important contribution towards the easing of labour shortages in particular industries has also been made by the bulk recruitment of foreign workers under schemes sponsored by the Ministry, as for instance the recruitment described in Chapter II of Italian men and women and ex-members of the Polish Armed Forces under British Command.

Distribution of Industry

Statutory responsibility for the distribution of industry rests, under the Distribution of Industry Acts, 1945 and 1950, with the Board of Trade which acts in consultation with the Treasury, the Ministry of Labour, the Ministry of Housing and Local Government and other interested Departments. The Ministry of Labour provides detailed information about employment and unemployment in areas under consideration and about the type and distribution of the labour force in the area, and draws attention to factors in the local situation likely to affect employment prospects. Under the Distribution of Industry Acts a number of areas where unemployment was exceptionally severe and prolonged before the war have been scheduled by the Board of Trade as Development Areas, and special action has been taken to assist their industrial development and diversification. These areas now include North-East England (including County Durham), Merseyside, the Wigan/St Helens district, North-East Lancashire, West Cumberland, South Wales and Monmouthshire, Wrexham, Clydeside, Dundee and part of the Scottish Highlands. In general, efforts are made to attract additional industry to these Development Areas and to other areas of comparatively high unemployment, and to reduce to a minimum additional demands for manpower in areas already short of labour. The Ministry keeps the Board of Trade generally informed on the local manpower position, and when a firm applies to the Board of Trade for permission to build or enlarge industrial premises in a particular area, the local employment situation is one of the factors considered by that Department when deciding whether or not Industrial Development Certificates should be issued. Where it appears that substantial unemployment may arise in any particular districts, the Ministry co-operates with other Government Departments in an attempt to increase the employment opportunities in the areas concerned, for example by ensuring that, as far as possible, government contracts are placed in areas with a surplus of labour. The Ministry also keeps other Government Departments concerned with economic policy fully informed on the employment (and unemployment) situation.

All of these activities can be properly performed only if accurate and up-to-date information on employment and unemployment is available, and areas of labour surplus and shortage can readily be identified. The regional offices of the Ministry therefore obtain from the local offices regular reports on employment and unemployment in their areas, the extent of short-time and overtime working and the present state and future prospects of local industries. The regional offices summarise this information for the Ministry's headquarters, and give an appraisement of the significance to be attached to statistical variations in the light of local knowledge. The statistical information collected from the local offices about unemployment and vacancies is supplemented by employment returns from employers. At the same time other Government Departments keep the Ministry informed of policies and developments likely to affect employment. In this way a detailed but comprehensive picture is built up, giving to those framing policy a full knowledge of its implications for employment.

Mobility of Labour

The White Paper on Employment Policy proposed that, in addition to the better distribution of industry, the problem of local unemployment should be met in two ways. One way was the removal of obstacles to the transfer of workers from one area to another, and from one occupation to another, and the other was the provision of training facilities to fit workers from declining industries for jobs in expanding industries. The importance of mobility of labour to reduce the short-term unemployment of those changing jobs, or temporarily unemployed for some other reason, was also stressed.

The Ministry has put these proposals into effect by providing vocational training schemes (which are dealt with in a later chapter) and giving financial assistance towards the transfer of labour. This assistance may include the payment of fares, lodging allowances for those away from home and maintaining a family in the home area, or grants to meet the cost of household removal. Apart from such special schemes of financial assistance, it has always been the practice to make advances of fares (usually by travelling warrant) to those travelling to employment found for them by the Employment Exchange. Such an advance is made against an undertaking to repay obtained from the employer or the worker. If the worker is qualified to receive unemployment benefit under the National Insurance Act, part of the cost is met from the National Insurance Fund. Welfare arrangements, which include assistance in making travel arrangements and in finding suitable accommodation, have also been made to help to ease the personal difficulties of workers transferred to other areas.

The Employment Exchange Service

The main function of the employment service is to try to find a suitable job as quickly as possible for each person registering for work, and to help employers notifying vacancies to find workers suitable for their requirements—in other words, to get the right person in the right job at the right time. This is a continuing task and it is never possible to secure the ideal distribution of labour owing to the constantly changing priorities. The specialised employment services of the Ministry's local offices are described in later chapters of this book, and the organisation of Employment Exchanges is described in Chapter XVI.

Certain basic principles have been laid down by the Ministry for the officers of the Employment Exchanges who are engaged on the work of registering men and women seeking employment and attempting to place them in suitable jobs. Anyone, employed or unemployed, may register for employment. Unemployed insured contributors must do so when they make a claim to unemployment benefit; others are registered as non-claimants. The basic principle governing the selection of persons for submission to a vacancy is that the best qualified persons on the register should be submitted without regard to irrelevant considerations such as race, colour, sex or belief. It is by keeping closely to the principle of suitability that the exchanges endeavour to gain and keep the confidence of employers and of those seeking work. Subject to this general principle, preference is given among equally well-qualified applicants to unemployed persons over persons already in employment, and workers are not brought into the district from farther afield if there are suitably qualified local workers. So far as possible, it is the practice to submit a number of candidates to the employer for his consideration so that he can make the final choice himself, just as a range of vacancies is available to the worker to choose from. In the conditions of full employment which have existed since the war, this is often not practicable. Finally, particular attention is given to employment which, at any one time, is of special importance in the national interest. The employment officer tries to persuade a worker who is suitable for work of particular national importance to choose this in preference to other work, but the freedom of the worker to make his own choice is fully respected and, more-over, no attempt is made to persuade him to take a job which does not make full use of his capabilities or which is clearly uncongenial to him.

The employer notifying a vacancy is responsible for deciding the rate of wages and the working conditions to be offered, and normally the function of the exchange is simply to report these accurately to applicants so that they can decide whether the vacancy suits their requirements. The local office cannot, of course, deal with a vacancy which appears to contravene the law. In certain industries minimum wages are determined by statute under the Wages Councils Acts, 1945 to 1948, or the Catering Wages Act, 1943, while in industry generally hours of employment and certain conditions may be governed by the Factories Acts, 1937 to 1948, the Shops Act, 1950, or similar legislation. If the conditions of the vacancy appear to violate the provisions of legislation, the exchange manager will point this out to the employer and tell him that unless there is an assurance that the wages or conditions will conform with the law, the exchange cannot deal with the vacancy.

There may also be difficulties when vacancies are notified in establishments affected by trade disputes. When Labour Exchanges were established in 1910, trade unions were anxious to know what action would be taken in these circumstances, and the Government wished to show that the system would work impartially towards employers and workers alike. The procedure eventually agreed, which remains in force, is that the employer's vacancies are dealt with in the ordinary way but a worker is informed by the local office that the vacancy is in work which is subject to an industrial dispute,

E

and he is perfectly free to refuse the offer of such a vacancy even though he may be in receipt of unemployment benefit or National Assistance. His title to this benefit or assistance will not be affected by his refusal of the vacancy.

When a man comes to an Employment Exchange to find work, the employment officer interviews him to obtain the information necessary to match the individual to the requirements of a job. A brief record is made of the inquirer's qualifications and experience and his requirements and preferences are discussed with him and also recorded. The employment officer then registers the inquirer for employment according to the occupation, or occupations, for which he appears to be most suitable. Likely vacancies currently available are discussed and, if possible, the registrant is given an introduction to one or more of the firms concerned. If no suitable vacancy is immediately available, the employment officer keeps the registration constantly under review, looking for freshly notified vacancies that may be suitable, and in appropriate cases making special approaches to local employers or sending particulars of the registrant to other Employment Exchanges.

When an employer asks the Employment Exchange to submit workers to him for a vacant job the employment officer examines the registration details of workers registered for employment and seeks those whose qualifications match those which the employer requires. If possible, he submits a selection of suitable persons, for the employer to decide which one to engage. If there are no suitable local registrants, the employment officer will seek the aid of neighbouring Employment Exchanges; if they cannot help, he will send details of the vacancy to his regional office, which will arrange for them to be circulated to other Employment Exchanges throughout a wider area, throughout the region or throughout the country. In this way a wider field of choice than the local one is opened both to those looking for work and to employers. When an employer agrees to accept a candidate from another area, arrangements may be made with the employer for the advance to the candidate of the fare for interview and for subsequent transfer. If the worker is eligible for grant-aided transfer, under one of the schemes designed to prevent or alleviate unemployment, the employment officer will give him full information concerning these, and will assist him, if necessary, in making the application for a grant. The employment officer in the area to which the worker is transferred will make any necessary arrangements for lodging accommodation.

To assist employment officers in their work of matching the requirements of employers and workers as speedily and effectively as possible, an occupational classification code has been devised.

The code groups related occupations under a main classification number which is divided further into sub-classification numbers. For each sub-classification, the main occupational terms and a short general definition of the duties which a person describing himself by one of those terms would normally perform are given; there is also, in each sub-classification, a list of the questions which should be asked by the employment officer to elicit the technical or occupational information needed to give an adequate picture of a registrant's skills or qualifications. The code is only an aid, however, to the relation of labour supply and demand and is intended to be used against the background of industrial knowledge which employment officers must acquire.

With one exception, it has not been found necessary to have special exchanges to deal with particular classes of vacancies or workers. In the hotel and catering industry, many hotel posts are residential and employers often have to go farther afield than their local areas to recruit staff. Since November, 1930, the Hotel and Catering Trades Exchange in Denmark Street, W.C.2, has given a special service to this industry both by serving the large number of hotel and catering employers and workers in Central London and by acting as a clearing house for registrants and vacancies in an area covering the southern half of England and Wales. A subsidiary clearing house attached to the Liverpool Employment Exchange provides a similar service for the northern half of England and Wales and another attached to Glasgow (Central) Exchange serves Scotland. If local employment cannot be found immediately, local offices forward particulars of experienced workers who are prepared to transfer away from home to the Denmark Street Exchange or to one of the clearing houses. Similarly, vacancies notified to local offices are referred to that exchange or to a clearing house.

Men and women seeking commercial work frequently register at local offices in the urban centres where their kind of work is concentrated, and in many of which a special commercial section has been established in the Employment Exchange. Should it be more convenient for such a registrant to apply to his local exchange, arrangements can be made for details of his experience and requirements to be sent to any other office known to have a wider range of vacancies in the commercial field.

In addition to matching men and women registered for employment against specific requirements notified by employers, employment officers are able to give information on employment opportunities in their own and other areas. They deal with inquiries on a wide range of professions and careers such as are covered in the *Careers Guide: Opportunities in the Professions and in Business Management* and in the "Choice of Careers" booklets referred to in the next chapter of this book.

There are two main reasons why the Ministry wishes to see the Employment Exchange service used to the fullest possible extent. The possibility of matching the skill and experience required by employers with that of the workers available is greater when a wide range of both jobs and workers is available, and so is the possibility of influencing, without statutory control, the distribution of man-power in accordance with the needs of the national economy. In each of the two years immediately before the war the number of men and women placed in employment by the service was about 2,150,000. In the early post-war period, the total was substantially higher, but it was influenced by the Control of Engagement Order, 1947, and later by the Notification of Vacancies Order, 1952. It has since fallen and in 1957 was about $1\frac{1}{2}$ million.

Higher Appointments

The services dealing with higher appointments are a comparatively recent development of the employment service. The original Appointments Service, which functioned after the First World War, had ceased in 1925. It provided a specialised employment and advisory service for those seeking professional, administrative, managerial and executive posts, including professional scientists and engineers, and for employers who needed staff of these kinds.

Another Appointments Service began in the Second World War and during the period of demobilisation it administered resettlement schemes for a large number of young men and women returning from the Armed Forces or changing over from war-time to peace-time occupations. This phase ended with the closing of the Appointments Offices, for economy reasons, at the end of March, 1957. The services for dealing with higher appointments now comprise the Technical and Scientific Register, the Professional and Executive Register and the Nursing Appointments Service.

The Technical and Scientific Register is centralised in London, and provides a national employment and advisory service for scientists and professionally qualified engineers, architects, estate agents and surveyors. There is a special unit which deals with the recruitment of highly qualified experts for under-developed countries under such schemes as the Colombo Plan and the United Nations Technical Assistance Scheme. The Register makes known to science and engineering graduates becoming available for National Service at the end of their studies, the opportunities in the Armed Forces and the arrangements under which indefinite deferment of National Service can be granted to such graduates. The Register is staffed by professionally qualified officers and on general policy matters is guided by the Technical Personnel Committee which functioned during the Second World War under the chairmanship of Lord Hankey. The Committee was reconstituted in 1951 under the chairmanship of Sir George Gater.

The work of placing other persons of professional, managerial and executive status is now carried out through the Employment Exchange service, and the Professional and Executive Register is held by 48 of the larger exchanges throughout the country. Although the Register is concerned mainly with men and women with professional qualifications or long business experience in responsible positions, it deals also with ex-regular officers of H.M. Forces and with young men and women of good education who may be particularly suitable for executive and managerial trainee posts in industry and commerce. Vacancies are circulated as required so that if necessary the field of selection of suitable candidates is extended to the whole country. Close co-operation exists between offices holding the Register and other local offices of the Ministry, at each of which there is a Liaison Officer to deal with inquiries about the Register. Contact is maintained with appropriate professional bodies.

The Appointments Service administers not only the Nursing Appointments Service described in Chapter II but also a business training scheme for ex-regular Servicemen and women under which suitable ex-regular officers and others are given the opportunity to acquire some business training. This may be by a course of theoretical or practical training or a combination of both. The theoretical courses are given at technical and commercial colleges and the practical training is provided in business firms. The Ministry pays the cost of tuition and textbooks and also makes a maintenance grant if the trainee's circumstances qualify him for it.

The Employment of Older Men and Women

In the preliminary survey of the Ministry in Chapter I, the problems of employing older men and women and of resettling ex-Regulars in civilian life was briefly referred to; both these problems are now discussed more fully.

In 1952, a National Advisory Committee, including representatives of the British Employers' Confederation, the Trades Union Congress, the Nationalised Industries, Government Departments, local authorities, welfare and other organisations, and experts in the medical and social science fields was appointed. In its first Report,[1] issued in

[1] First Report of the National Advisory Committee on the Employment of Older Men and Women (Cmd. 8963).

1953, the Committee recommended that employers should review any practices or agreements that place an age barrier in the way of older people seeking employment and should adopt a positive policy of giving older workers a fair chance to compete on their merits for available jobs; it also recommended that all employed men and women who could give effective service should be given the opportunity to continue at work without regard to age if they so wished. The Report was accepted by the Government and the Ministry arranged for its findings to be given wide publicity. The National Joint Advisory Council agreed to commend the Report to its constituent bodies for consideration.

Following the publication of this Report many employers have revised their engagement and retirement practices to provide greater opportunities. In December, 1955, the National Advisory Committee issued a second Report[1] which reviews the developments since the first Report appeared. It confirmed the soundness and practicability of the main statement of principles in the first Report and recorded that, although some progress had been made, there was room for a wider adoption of the recommendations previously made and for further experiments and research to meet particular difficulties. It emphasised the continuing need for firms to examine the age structure of their establishments and also the desirability of industries promoting research into those aspects of the employment of older workers that were their particular concern. This second Report was also endorsed by the National Joint Advisory Council.

The Resettlement of Ex-Regular Members of H.M. Forces

The resettlement in civilian life of ex-regular Servicemen and women has presented some difficulty. Skills and experience gained in the Forces have not always been recognised in civilian life, and men of experience and maturity have frequently had to enter civilian employment at a level below that which their ability deserved. This has resulted in a wastage of national manpower and has been to some extent a deterrent to those considering a career in the Forces. The Ministry has given special consideration to this problem. In 1948 an Inter-Departmental Committee was formed to seek a solution and co-ordinate action, and in 1950 an Advisory Council— on the Relationship between Employment in the Services and Civilian Life—was set up to advise the Minister of Labour and National Service and the Minister of Defence jointly on the best ways of integrating experience gained in the Services into civilian

---

[1] Second Report of the National Advisory Committee on the Employment of Older Men and Women (Cmd. 9628).

life. With the Council's approval the Ministry asked the main industries and the chief commercial organisations for their co-operation to consider ways of giving ex-Regulars opportunities for suitable employment. As a result, many employers have agreed to fill some of their vacancies by recruiting ex-Regulars or to relax age-limits in their favour. In some cases they have given preference to ex-Regulars for certain kinds of jobs or trained them at the firm's own expense. After discussions between the Service Departments and the trade unions, Service training in most trades is recognised for membership of trade unions. To help those whose Service work has no direct equivalent in civilian life, the Ministry has set up various training schemes.[1] Although many of the older ex-officers still find it hard to get suitable civilian employment, these various measures have made the resettlement of ex-Regulars in civilian life much easier.

A further complication was introduced in 1957 when it was announced that the new defence plan would inevitably mean that some regular officers and N.C.O.s would have to retire prematurely. To meet this situation the Minister of Labour, after consulting the Advisory Council, appointed a small Board representing both sides of industry and commerce to advise him on the measures to be taken. Subsequently Resettlement Committees, constituted on similar lines to the Board, were set up in Scotland and Wales and each of the Ministry's administrative regions in England. In addition the existing agencies concerned with resettlement—the Ministry of Labour, the Services and the voluntary associations—were linked more closely together in a Regular Forces Resettlement Service. A retired senior Air Force officer was appointed Director of Resettlement. All these measures were designed to increase the opportunities for Regulars, both officers and men, to make effective use of their abilities when they leave the Forces.

Co-operation with Industry

The Ministry frequently seeks the advice of the National Joint Advisory Council on employment matters, and may ask the Council to consider policy proposals and to assist in securing their general acceptance. If the Council endorses the policy proposed, the members representing the British Employers' Confederation, the Trades Union Congress and the Nationalised Industries recommend it to their constituent bodies, who in turn inform their members. Recommendations, as appropriate, are also referred by the Ministry to its local advisory Committees and many of these Committees initiate

[1] These schemes were revised with the advice of the Resettlement Advisory Board.

local action to bring the recommendations to the notice of employers and interested bodies and to enlist their co-operation.

The work of the Ministry in connection with employment is unlikely to change substantially while the present economic situation exists, and its main tasks will probably continue to be concerned with increasing the supply of labour and ensuring its best distribution in the national interest, increasing its mobility and improving the employment prospects of such sections of the community as the older workers and the ex-regular Servicemen.

CHAPTER IV

The Youth Employment Service

*

YOUNG persons are always of prime importance to the nation as they are the raw material from which the craftsmen, technicians, executives and managers of tomorrow are moulded and on which the future of our industry, commerce and the professions depends. The fall in the birth-rate in the late 1920's and the early 1930's has resulted in a scarcity of young people since the end of the war. There was a decline, for example, of one-third between 1939 and 1954 in the number of persons under 21 years of age available for employment. This scarcity has enhanced the need to ensure that the available supply of new entrants to employment is used in the best possible way. There will, however, be a substantial increase after 1958 in the number of young persons available, reaching a peak in 1962 and declining rapidly thereafter. This is familiarly known as 'the bulge' and will affect the employment position in the youth field for the next few years.

The right choice of employment is of the greatest importance. The happiness and well-being of the individual depend very considerably on the opportunity to use his abilities on a congenial and suitable job which offers good training, good working conditions and a chance to progress as skill and experience increase. In an economy demanding a high level of productivity, the zest which a happy worker brings to his job is also important. The national cost of education is high and in the interests of all—school-leavers, parents and employers—it is desirable that the knowledge and training gained at school should not be wasted in the succeeding years but should be applied and widened. The State therefore provides a Youth Employment Service to advise boys and girls leaving school on their choice of career, to assist them to find a suitable job, and to be available for further advice should the need arise.

When the post-war services of the Ministry were planned, the Youth Employment Service came under review. A Committee representing educational, industrial and administrative interests was appointed under the chairmanship of the Permanent Secretary to the Ministry to define the central functions of the service and make recommendations as to how it should be administered.

The Labour Exchanges Act, 1909, and the Education (Choice of Employment) Act, 1910, had resulted in the responsibility for choice of employment work being divided both centrally and locally. This dual responsibility created difficulties which were increased when the Unemployment Insurance Act, 1920, placed upon the Minister of Labour the responsibility in matters relating to unemployment for juveniles in all areas. The Government therefore referred the whole question for independent examination, in 1920, by Lord Chelmsford, and again in 1925, by a Committee presided over by Mr (later Sir) Dougal O. Malcolm. Lord Chelmsford recommended that education authorities exercising choice of employment powers should also administer unemployment insurance; but he left the difficult question of the division of central responsibility unsolved. The Malcolm Committee recommended that duality at the centre should cease and the responsibility should rest on the Minister of Labour; but that duality in local administration should remain. Since 1927 that has been the pattern of administration of the Youth Employment Service. With the passing of years weaknesses in the system became apparent. For example, the undertaking given by the Minister, in 1927, to allow education authorities scope to develop the work on individual lines had the effect of denying the Minister sufficient authority over the whole field to ensure common standards of efficiency. There was too much division into small areas, and an education authority might at any time take over the work from the Minister, and later give it up at three months' notice—with disruptive effect on the service.

The arrangements for the administration of the service were not within the terms of reference of what is called the Ince Committee. The Committee nevertheless recorded that, if it had been able to agree upon a single system of local administration, whether by the Ministry or by local authorities, it would have felt justified in recommending accordingly. In the absence of such agreement, its recommendations were designed to ensure smoother and more effective working of the existing dual system. It recommended that the new service should be administered at the centre jointly by the Minister of Labour and National Service, the Minister of Education and the Secretary of State for Scotland, but that the Minister of Labour should continue to be responsible to Parliament. Local education authorities (education authorities, in Scotland) should be given a once-for-all option of providing the service in their areas, and where they chose to do so the Ministry of Labour and National Service should continue to pay them a grant-in-aid; in the remaining areas the service should be provided by the Ministry of Labour and National Service.

The Committee's main recommendations were accepted. Some were put into effect immediately by administrative action; others were embodied in the Employment and Training Act, 1948. The effect was to widen the scope of the service, provide a new central body of a somewhat novel character for its administration, and remedy the previous weaknesses in the arrangements made for local administration by education authorities. These were required by the Act to give notice within a certain period that they proposed to provide a Youth Employment Service, and after the specified periods expired their right to make such a proposal lapsed. If a local education authority desired to exercise powers it has to do so for the whole of its area. The Act conferred these powers on authorities in Scotland for the first time.

The Youth Employment Service is responsible not only for vocational guidance, placing and after care, but also for the provision of information on which the choice of employment can be based; it encourages industries to set up national schemes, agreed between employers' and workers' representatives, for the recruitment, training and employment of young persons; and it administers a training allowances scheme providing maintenance grants in certain circumstances for young persons living away from home.

The Minister is advised by a national council—the National Youth Employment Council—which has separate Advisory Committees for Scotland and Wales; the Council and Committees are appointed on a statutory basis for a three-year period. Membership is drawn from representatives of employers and workers, education authorities and teachers in the various types of secondary schools and includes also a number of independent members interested in youth welfare.

The new central administrative body, the Central Youth Employment Executive, which was set up under the Employment and Training Act, 1948, is responsible to the Minister for youth employment policy and procedure. Its Chairman is an officer of the Ministry of assistant secretary rank and its members, of principal officer or equivalent rank, consist of a representative of the Ministry of Education (who is also secretary to the National Youth Employment Council) one of the Scottish Education Department and two of the Ministry. With the exception of the Scottish representative, each of the members is also responsible for the work of a division of the Ministry's youth employment branch; the Scottish representative, stationed in his own Department in Edinburgh, advises on policy affecting education authorities and other educational bodies in

Scotland. The Executive meets formally at frequent intervals and there is also day-to-day informal contact. An administrative body consisting of representatives of three Government Departments working together is a new development in administration. So far it can be said that the experiment has been a success.

The Executive issues information on careers in the form of booklets, memoranda and, to a limited extent, films. The booklets in the 'Choice of Careers' series, published by H.M. Stationery Office, contain general information on professions, industries, occupations and services; for each subject they describe the main practices and features, methods of recruitment and training, conditions of employment, facilities for further education and the prospects before the young entrant. Over 80 booklets have been issued, many have been revised on reprint, and many more are in preparation.

Education authorities which provide the service in their areas do so in accordance with a scheme approved in each case by the Minister. The scheme sets out in detail the organisation of the service and is an undertaking by the authority to provide an efficient service in the manner indicated. An estimate of its proposed expenditure upon the service is submitted annually to the Minister by every authority, and 75 per cent of the approved expenditure is paid by the Ministry.

The Central Youth Employment Executive also has its own inspectorate. The system of inspection is a valuable means of ensuring that the service is guided in matters of policy and procedure; its purpose is to satisfy the Minister that public money is being well spent. In practice, the inspectors approach their task with the intention of giving the fullest possible advice and help to those responsible for the conduct of the service, and of ensuring that methods which have proved their worth are made known as widely as possible. Visits of inspection are paid to the youth employment offices of local education authorities and to youth employment departments in local offices of the Ministry. In these inspections an H.M. Inspector of Schools is always associated with one of the Executive's inspectors. When the formal survey of the work is complete, the inspectors discuss their findings with the Chief Education Officer or the Regional Controller, as the case may be, and prepare a joint report for the Minister. In addition, the inspectors may make informal visits to follow up recommendations made in a report and generally to keep in touch with the progress of the service.

Local Administration

Representatives of the Central Youth Employment Executive have been appointed at each of the Ministry's nine regional offices and at its Scottish and Welsh Headquarters, and are available for day-to-day consultation with local education authorities and youth employment officers. Their duties include the constant review of the development of the service in their region, co-ordination of its work and the promotion of training for its staff.

Since 1910, Youth Employment Committees have played an important part in the local administration of the Youth Employment Service. Where the service is operated by an education authority, the members of the Committee are appointed by, and are advisory to, their local authority. In other areas they are appointed by the Minister to advise him and their membership follows the pattern of the national council. In many areas, members of these Committees give practical assistance in following up the progress of boys and girls who have started work.

The facilities offered by the service are the same whether they are provided by a local authority or by the Ministry. The procedure for registration and placing in employment is, in general, similar to that described in the previous chapter.

The Work of the Youth Employment Officer

To do his job properly the youth employment officer must, like the employment officer in the exchange, have a good knowledge of industry and occupations. But he studies these from the more particular viewpoint of the method of recruitment and training of youth; the day-to-day work on the job; the technical classes needed to supplement the practical training; the examinations to be passed; the prospects for the new entrant and the usual avenues of progress. He needs to be in constant contact with the firms in his area, visiting them to see what is required in the various jobs and following up the progress of boys and girls whom he has placed. He learns a great deal from this follow-up of progress, and all this knowledge and experience is brought into use when the time comes to match boys and girls leaving school with the jobs which have become available for them.

If the youth employment officer is to find the most suitable jobs for individual school-leavers, he must have some means of knowing their abilities, aptitudes and achievements. There is statutory provision for this, and schools are required to furnish confidential school-leaving reports on all pupils leaving school at the statutory minimum school-leaving age. Such reports give information on the school-leaver's health, educational attainments, general ability and special aptitudes and they are open to inspection by the parents if they wish to see them. Nearly every boy and girl for whom a report is received is given an individual interview before leaving school.

The programme of school-leaving interviews is planned in advance each term by the youth employment officer in co-operation with the head teacher or the careers staff of the schools in the area.

Most boys and girls entering their last year at school have already begun to think about the kind of job that they would like to obtain. Some hope to learn a skilled trade; some are concerned only with the money they will earn and how they will spend it; others think chiefly in terms of security. The majority have only a vague idea of the range of work open to them or of the qualifications and abilities needed to do the different types of job well. The visit to the school of the youth employment officer to give a talk about these matters is, therefore, of importance and interest to them. From him (or her) they hear how main groups of jobs fit in with the main types of boys and girls and how important it is that in the chosen job the new-comers should have a chance to develop their abilities and interests; they are also urged to take a longer view than the immediate future—to think less of the money they will earn when they start work and more of the salary and the position in the community they will later command through their experience and skill. In the months before they leave school they have the opportunity of reading 'Choice of Careers' booklets and they may see some of the 'choice of employment' films, visit factories or workshops in the area or hear talks on particular occupations or professions. The school-leaver is thus in a position to make a more informed choice when the time comes for the youth employment officer to have a talk with him and his parents. At this interview the youth employment officer advises the boy or girl on the kind of job he thinks will be most suitable. Sometimes a school-leaver has made up his mind beforehand about the kind of job he is going to take, and his decision is not a wise one; it is often possible at the school-leaving interview to suggest an alternative and more suitable plan. When a choice is made the youth employment officer helps, if necessary, to find a suitable opening.

The youth employment officer in an area where employment is plentiful and varied has a vastly different job from that of his colleagues in remote and thinly populated areas. In remote rural areas a boy or girl with even outstanding aptitudes had at one time little chance of finding employment in which they could be used. The training allowances scheme administered by the Ministry seeks to remedy this. One example of how the scheme works, chosen out of many, is that of a boy of 17 years of age in a rural area who, having taken examinations which entitled him to exemption from the London University inter-B.Sc. examination, had set his heart on a career in aeronautics. The headmaster reported that this boy had outstanding ability and character and was already a member of the

Air Britain Association. As there was no chance locally of any kind of engineering training, let alone training in aeronautical engineering, the boy was recommended for a grant under the training allowances scheme and was placed as an apprentice in a famous firm of aeronautical engineers. Such boys and girls generally justify the chance given them. In the case quoted, the boy gained first prize for the best all-round work of the first-year technical apprentices.

Another set of problems faces the youth employment officer when he comes to consider how boys and girls with a physical or mental handicap can be given the chance of learning work in which they can successfully compete with others of their age and ultimately become self-supporting. In such cases, the youth employment officer works in close collaboration not only with the head teachers (including those in special schools) but also with the disablement resettlement officer of the Employment Exchange, whose work will be described in the next chapter, and with the other statutory and voluntary bodies with responsibilities in this field.

The youth employment officer continues to take an interest in the progress of young people after employment has begun. This is an important part of the service, for no matter how good the preparation may have been for the transition from school to work, difficulty and misunderstanding may occur. After a suitable settling-in period, the youth employment officer invites those who have been placed in work to come to an 'open evening' held on a set day and at a set time each week. One or two members of the Youth Employment Committee may be present with the youth employment officer to meet the young workers. In the majority of cases those who come are getting on satisfactorily; some may need to have their difficulties explained to them from the work point of view and so are helped to settle down; a few may be advised to seek another job. A case in which a change seemed advisable was that of a boy with good educational qualifications and an interest in science and engineering, whose parents did not wish him to enter engineering employment because there was a recession in the motor industry—the main industry offering such employment locally—at the time when he left school. He took a job as a sales assistant in a bookshop, but was not happy in this work. At an 'opening evening' a few months later the youth employment officer discussed other possibilities with him, and advised him to discuss them with his parents; as a result he was successfully placed, with their consent, in an opening as a scientific assistant. At these 'open evenings' boys and girls, and especially those away from home, are advised on leisure activities as well as on work; on suitable youth clubs to join where they can enjoy their favourite pastimes, or on technical classes where they can pursue some subject in which they are interested. Questions are also answered on a variety of subjects such as the effect of apprenticeship on family allowances and the financial assistance available for attendance at technical classes. A careful watch is kept on the progress of boys and girls who have come to an area from distant homes and the good offices of the welfare officers in the firms concerned are specially enlisted. Special care is taken, too, in cases brought to the notice of the youth employment officer by the probation officer; the boy or girl is often only too glad to have a second chance and to 'turn over a new leaf'.

The difficulties of the youth employment officer are, of course, not always solved successfully. Everyone in this country is free to reject advice, whether good or bad, and not every boy and girl desires advice on the choice of employment and not everyone is willing to take the advice given; many learn by way of trial and error. In areas of full employment there is sometimes no opportunity to advise at the time of a change of job as, in such areas, fresh jobs are secured easily and often without recourse to the Youth Employment Service.

The Training of Youth Employment Officers

The youth employment officer is not only a civil servant or a local government officer—he is also a social worker. The work is of an exacting nature and proper training is of the greatest importance. A Committee was set up in 1949 under the chairmanship of Lord Piercy to consider this problem, and it recommended a full-time training course lasting one year. For reasons of economy it has not yet been possible to implement this recommendation. A one-year course has been provided at Lamorbey Park since 1949 by the Kent Local Education Authority, which supplies annually up to 25 recruits to the service. In 1955 a three-week course, provided by the Central Youth Employment Executive, was held at Birkbeck College, London. A similar course, lasting four weeks, has been held in each subsequent year. In addition, several short courses in the basic work of vocational guidance are held each year throughout the country.

The Development of the Service

Since 1947 a modern service has been built up on what was good in the foundations of the old; a period of gradual development and consolidation has followed. Before the passing of the Employment and Training Act in 1948, 68 local education authorities in England and Wales exercised choice of employment powers. The Act allowed authorities until January, 1949, to decide whether to exercise these powers in future, and 128 out of 181 authorities in Great Britain now do so. In many areas, during the years immediately after the passing of the Act, arrangements had to be made for the transfer of responsibility for the local operation of the service from the Ministry to education authorities. New premises had to be acquired and new staff recruited and trained.

By the end of 1950 the reorganisation was almost complete and it has since been possible to turn attention to developing and improving the service. Despite the need for economy good progress has been made. New procedures have been tested and the activities of the service widened. The partnerships between the three Departments, centrally, and between education authorities and the officers of the Ministry, locally, have been fostered and strengthened. As the experience of youth employment officers has increased the service has become more effective and more widely used. In recent years the important part which the service has to play has become increasingly recognised by employers, teachers, young persons, and their parents.

Two particular problems will exercise the service in the comparatively near future. One is the need to improve and extend the facilities which are offered to the older school-leaver. The other, already mentioned, is the rise in the school-leaving population which began in 1957 and which, for the country as a whole, will reach a peak 50 per cent above the 1956 figure in 1962. The increase in the school-leaving population will create many problems, but the service is now sufficiently developed to be able to meet and resolve them.

F

CHAPTER V

Service for the Disabled

*

A SOURCE of manpower that has been made use of to an increasing extent during the period of scarcity since the end of the war has been the disabled. The work which the Ministry is called upon to do in rehabilitating and resettling the disabled is both of value to the nation and of help to the individual disabled person.

Although special measures had been taken by the Government after the end of the 1914–18 war to assist disabled persons to secure employment (including the introduction of the King's National Roll Scheme to encourage employers to take on a percentage of disabled ex-Servicemen), a comprehensive state service was not developed until after the beginning of the Second World War. In 1941, the Minister, Mr Ernest Bevin, in association with the Health Departments, introduced an 'Interim Scheme for the Training and Resettlement of Disabled Persons'. Later in the year, a Committee under the chairmanship of Mr George Tomlinson, Joint Parliamentary Secretary to the Ministry, was appointed to make recommendations for a permanent service and these recommendations were incorporated in the Disabled Persons (Employment) Act, 1944.

The provisions of the Act were based on the assumption that if care were taken in assessing individual capacity and in selecting employment, and if special aids were supplied where necessary, the great majority of disabled persons could take their place in industry on equal terms with the able-bodied, and some of the remainder could do useful work if employed under sheltered conditions. Under the Interim Scheme the Ministry had already set up a disablement resettlement officer service which could make a systematic contact between the hospital service and the employment service and the Act established this on a permanent basis. It also provided for the voluntary registration of disabled persons, for an obligation on employers of 20 or more workers to employ a quota of persons so registered, and for the designation of certain occupations to be reserved solely for the disabled; it gave sanction for industrial rehabilitation and vocational training services and, where necessary, for training and employment of the more severely disabled to be given under sheltered conditions.

Under the Act, the Minister appointed a National Advisory Council on the Employment of the Disabled to advise him in matters relating to the services for the disabled. On the Council there are representatives of employers' and of workers' organisations in equal numbers, medical representatives, and others with particular interest and experience in the problems of disablement. The first Chairman of the Council was Lord Ridley. From 1947 to 1955 Sir Brunel Cohen was Chairman, when his place was taken by Sir Harold Wiles, a former Deputy Secretary of the Ministry. Much of the work of the Council is done through four Committees which deal with special aspects of the disablement problem; these are the Blind Persons Committee, the Medical Committee, the Training and Employment Committee, and the Sheltered Employment Committee.

Nearly 300 local Disablement Advisory Committees were also set up throughout the country to advise the Minister through his local offices on the general problems of disablement in their areas and to assist in an executive capacity in the administration of the Act. Membership is on a basis similar to that of the National Advisory Council. Individual cases are referred to the Committees in certain circumstances by the local disablement resettlement officers; for example, there may be doubt about an application for registration, a complaint that an employer has unreasonably discharged a disabled person, or an application from an employer for a reduction in the quota of disabled persons he is required to employ. Most of these cases are examined by special panels of the Committees whose recommendations are usually accepted by the local officer; if a recommendation cannot be accepted the local officer refers it to his regional office for a decision or for further reference to headquarters.

The purpose of registration under the Act is to identify disabled persons who are able to benefit from its employment provisions—the quota, designated employment, and the special employment and training facilities provided for the severely disabled. The main conditions for inclusion in the register are that the applicant's disablement within the meaning of the Act is likely to last for at least six months,[1] and that he has a reasonable prospect of obtaining and keeping some form of paid work. No application may be rejected before it has been referred to the local Disablement Advisory Committee for a recommendation. By 1950 the number registered

---

[1] This period is shortly to be altered to one year.

had risen to 940,000, but since then there has been a gradual decline. In October 1957 the total was 750,000.

Only two occupations, those of passenger electric lift attendant and of car park attendant, have been designated under the Act as occupations expressly reserved for the disabled.

The quota requirement applies to all employers of 20 or more workers, and the standard percentage of disabled persons who must be employed is at present 3 per cent of the total staff. With few exceptions, employers have accepted their quota obligations willingly and with a real wish to fulfil them, but although the compulsory quota helps, it by no means solves the problem of placing the disabled in employment. Successful placing work must also depend on the ability of the disablement resettlement officer to satisfy employers that the engagement of suitable disabled persons can be justified on normal employment considerations.

Because of the size and complexity of the rehabilitation problem and the number of Government Departments concerned, a Standing Rehabilitation and Resettlement Committee was appointed, as recommended by the Tomlinson Committee, to co-ordinate departmental work on behalf of the disabled and to exercise some supervision over developments. The Chairman and secretary are provided by the Ministry and the members are drawn from the Ministries of Education, Health, Labour and National Service, Pensions and National Insurance, the National Assistance Board, the corresponding Scottish Departments and the Government of Northern Ireland.

The Disablement Resettlement Officer Service of the Employment Exchanges

On the staff of every Employment Exchange there is at least one disablement resettlement officer, generally known as the 'D.R.O.' These officers are specially selected and trained, and are responsible for advising disabled men and women and assisting them in securing employment. In a small Employment Exchange the D.R.O. is often also the supervisor of the general employment section, but in the larger exchanges there is a separate disablement resettlement section of which he has charge. Every D.R.O. works in close co-operation with the other employment officers and is kept informed of all the vacancies notified to the exchange. The part-time D.R.O. can call upon the Group D.R.O., who is a full-time officer, for advice and assistance.

Any disabled person, whether registered under the Act or not, who is in need of employment or advice on employment problems may ask for a private interview with the D.R.O. Arrangements exist under which the D.R.O. may obtain expert medical advice on the capabilities of the disabled person, the conditions under which he ought to be employed, and the environmental factors which would be unsuitable in view of the disability. The D.R.O. also visits hospitals and other medical institutions to interview and advise patients about to be discharged with a residual disablement. This gives him an ideal first contact with the disabled man or woman. Advice can be obtained at the same time from the medical staff who have been treating the patient and no time need be lost between medical recovery and the start of industrial rehabilitation. For exceptionally difficult cases, medical interviewing Committees have been set up in some hospitals to provide a more detailed medical assessment of the person's employment abilities. In increasing numbers hospitals arrange a case conference between the doctor, the almoner and the D.R.O.; this close co-operation between the hospitals and the service is steadily developing.

The D.R.O. tackles the problem of finding suitable employment from the point of view of a man's abilities rather than that of his disabilities. By training and experience, and with medical guidance where necessary, he has learnt to assess a disabled person's employment capacity.

Placing a disabled person in employment is much more a matter of seeking vacancies that will suit the individual than of trying to fit the individual into a notified vacancy, and the D.R.O. frequently makes a special approach to local employers to ask their help in difficult cases. Sometimes the matter is a relatively simple one; for example, of finding a man a job in his own occupation but in a workroom on the ground floor. Occasionally the needs of the D.R.O. fit in very happily with those of the employer as in one case where a very noisy power press was manned, at the suggestion of the D.R.O., by a man disabled through deafness. One of the most convincing proofs of the wisdom of the basic assumption of the Act is given by the residents of the Duchess of Gloucester House, Isleworth, the hostel administered by the Ministry[1] for men and women disabled by paraplegia but who go out to full-time ordinary employment in the neighbourhood. These people, whose spinal cord injuries have deprived them of movement below the point of fracture, have invalid chairs for indoor use and motor-cars or motorised chairs for outdoor use. The local D.R.O. has found them suitable sedentary employment in nearby factories and offices and there, working side by side with their able-bodied colleagues, they are able to compete successfully and on their merits.

[1] The Home was set up in 1949 by the Ministry of Pensions and administered by it until August, 1953.

Rehabilitation

Many people who have been sick or injured need rehabilitation courses to fit them either physically, or psychologically, or both, to resume their employment or to begin vocational training for new work. In addition to those who have been ill or injured, there are some permanently disabled people who have had a long period of unemployment and can be helped by a rehabilitation course to adapt themselves to working conditions again. It is for such men and women that the Ministry provides courses of industrial rehabilitation, and from the beginning of the scheme in 1943 to the end of 1957 over 87,000 men and women have been helped in this way.

The first industrial rehabilitation unit was set up in 1943 at Egham in Surrey and nearly 15,000 men and women have completed a course there since then. It has room for 200 residents. The proved value of its work led to the opening of 14 more units in various parts of the country. These have each a capacity of 100 and, except for the units at Leicester and Granton, Edinburgh, which take 50 and 35 boarders respectively, they are non-residential. They mainly serve the areas around them; those who live too far afield for daily travel either go to Egham, Leicester or Granton as residents or are found lodgings near one of the other units.

The course averages eight weeks in length and is intended to ensure that at the end of it a person can go to a full day's work or to training. Most of those entering the courses are submitted by hospitals or doctors, but D.R.O.s often recommend men and women with long-standing disabilities and some are sent by works doctors.

At each unit there are excellently equipped workshops provided with up-to-date machine tools, a gymnasium and a garden. The gymnasium and the garden are very useful for restoring physical fitness but the largest part of the work of rehabilitation is done in the workshops. In these, the busy atmosphere suggests the factory rather than the sick bay, and by working on tasks graduated to their growing capabilities, men and women recapture the readiness and confidence to work without fear of failure. In addition, they can try work outside their previous experience and, if necessary, revise their theoretical knowledge. During the course they are paid an allowance.

Each person has his own problems and anxieties and each is given the personal attention of the team of experts running the unit. There is a medical officer who looks after physical progress and safeguards; under his guidance a remedial gymnast supervises exercises suitable for those suffering from various disabilities. A vocational psychologist assesses the potentialities of each person and these are further tested by the variety of work done in the workshops under the eye of skilled tradesmen. About five-sixths of those attending a course are advised to take up work different from that which they have done previously. A social worker helps to resolve personal and domestic troubles barring the way to resettlement. The team also includes a D.R.O., whose task is to try to have the right job ready for each person finishing a course. He does this by working in close co-operation with D.R.O.s in the areas where the jobs are available.

Each person who has completed a course is asked six months later what progress he is making. It has been found that about four-fifths start work within three months of leaving and that most of them are satisfied with their jobs. A typical example of a worker resettled with a change of occupation is that of a man aged 25, who worked as a farm labourer until he contracted tuberculosis of the hip. He spent five years in hospital and then a year at home before entering an industrial rehabilitation course. At first his left knee was very stiff and he needed two sticks for walking, but by the end of the course he had been able to discard them. He was found to be intelligent, and the vocational psychologist recommended training in clerical and commercial subjects. After the industrial rehabilitation course he took a training course in these subjects and is now working as a clerk.

In November, 1951, an Industrial Rehabilitation Development Committee was set up to keep under examination the Ministry's industrial rehabilitation policy. The members of the Committee include the Under-Secretary in the Ministry in charge of industrial rehabilitation and training, the Treasury Medical Adviser, and an occupational psychologist and a sociologist, both of the University of London. The Committee has made two Reports, one in 1952 and one in 1956. Resulting from a recommendation of the earlier Report, a research and development rehabilitation unit was opened at Waddon in Surrey in 1954. In the later Report the Committee recorded that there had grown up in the industrial rehabilitation units a reasonably uniform body of practices which had now proved their worth. The Committee welcomed certain developments— particularly the closer links with the regional medical service and with mental hospitals. It also noted the recent development of co-operation with the Youth Employment Service whereby the industrial rehabilitation units take young people who are presenting particularly difficult problems to the youth employment officer and give them a full vocational assessment lasting a few days.

Vocational Training

The Ministry also provides vocational training for the disabled as part of the general training facilities described in the next chapter.

At any one time there are normally more than 2,000 disabled persons in course of training who, wherever possible, are trained side-by-side with the able-bodied.

The disabled are given priority in two ways. Some courses, in trades which offer only a restricted field for the employment of adult trainees, are reserved entirely for the disabled; in others, where training vacancies are limited, all disabled ex-Servicemen and women are given priority irrespective of the date of their application and of the number of other applicants awaiting training. Other disabled persons receive equal priority with able-bodied ex-regular Servicemen and women who, in turn, are allocated to training in preference to other able-bodied persons. Before a disabled person is accepted for training a medical report is obtained and his capabilities, aptitudes and wishes are weighed in relation to employment opportunities. Special medical supervision is provided during training and, if necessary, the curriculum is adjusted or the length of the course extended; an example is the part-time training which has recently been introduced for disabled persons suffering from tuberculosis who are not yet fit for full-time training. For the more seriously disabled who are not able to travel daily from their homes to the training establishment or to stay in ordinary lodgings, the Ministry reserves places and pays the cost of training and maintenance, at Queen Elizabeth's Training College for the Disabled at Leatherhead, Surrey; St Loyes College, Exeter; Finchale Abbey, Durham; and Portland Training College, near Mansfield, which are residential centres provided by voluntary organisations.

In some circumstances grants are given to disabled persons of suitable ability to help them to undertake courses of training or study leading to the professions; such training must be for a recognised qualification and must meet the requirements of the chosen profession.

Between 1941 and 1957 over 60,000 disabled men and women satisfactorily completed vocational training and were placed in employment in their training trades. To give but one example of successful resettlement after training, hundreds of one-armed welders were trained in Government Training Centres and residential colleges and these men, using artificial fitments in place of their missing limbs, have been able to hold their own in industry.

Sheltered Employment and Training for the Severely Disabled

The Disabled Persons (Employment) Act, 1944, empowers the Minister to provide special training and employment facilities for the severely disabled who are unlikely to get work in industry under ordinary conditions. These special facilities may be provided by a company specially set up by the Minister for the purpose; or by voluntary associations or bodies with workshops approved by the Minister as suitable; or by local authorities acting within their statutory powers either directly or through the agency of voluntary associations. In the first case, the capital expenditure involved and any operating losses are met from public funds. In the other two cases the whole cost of training, including maintenance allowances to trainees, is paid by the Ministry: capital advances may be made to help in starting a scheme or in developing its existing facilities; in addition, grants are made to meet a proportion of all operating losses incurred. In all, about 12,000 men and women are given employment in this way. Of the total number of registered disabled persons only about one-half per cent are unemployed and unlikely to be able to undertake employment or work except under special conditions.

In April, 1945, a special non-profit-making company incorporated under the Companies Act, 1929, and now known as Remploy Limited, was set up by the Minister under the provisions of the Act. Its directors, who include a number of prominent business men and trade union officials, are appointed by the Minister. The company has established 90 factories giving sheltered employment to more than 6,000 severely disabled workers. The difficulties that had to be overcome in establishing these factories were formidable and very different from those that face an ordinary commercial concern; for example the location of factories could not be decided on economic grounds but was dependent on the number of severely disabled in an area for whom there was no other employment. None the less Remploy has made great progress in the 13 years of its existence and the scale of its activities can be judged from the fact that sales are now running at over £3 million a year.

Among the company's products are furniture, joinery and other woodwork, leatherwork, industrial clothing, light engineering work, tubular furniture, sheet metal work, surgical footwear, orthopaedic appliances, bookbinding and printing, knitted wear, cardboard boxes and packaging. The products are sold in the ordinary commercial market. Government Departments give the company a share of their orders at current prices for any articles it can produce and local authorities have been asked to do the same. Standard scales of wages fixed in agreement with the trade unions are paid to the employees irrespective of the trade on which they are engaged; but higher skill and production are recognised by the payment of higher rates. A few of the Remploy factories run home-worker schemes for severely disabled people who are confined to their homes, but the development of such schemes has been hampered by the difficulty of finding suitable work.

More than 30 voluntary organisations providing facilities for the training and employment of severely disabled persons have been recognised as qualifying for assistance under the Act. Ranging from workshops with several branches to small workshops catering for local needs they fulfil a most useful purpose, especially in helping to deal with small numbers of severely disabled persons in areas where the setting up of a Remploy factory would not be justified. Very few local authorities have so far set up sheltered workshops for the sighted but some have arrangements by which sighted persons may be employed in the special workshops provided for the blind.

Employment Problems Associated with Certain Disabilities

The arrangements for the training and employment of the blind differ from those for other disabled persons in that local authorities have a statutory responsibility for promoting their welfare, including the provision of sheltered employment. The Ministry, however, meets most of the cost of industrial rehabilitation and training and makes grants to local authorities towards the cost of providing and maintaining workshops for the blind and home-workers' schemes. The Ministry's officers co-operate with any specialist services provided by local authorities, or voluntary bodies acting on their behalf, for placing the blind in ordinary employment. In this field the opportunities for placing have been considerably widened in recent years.

The resettlement of tuberculous persons presents two main problems: the provision of training and employment facilities on a part-time basis during the long period of recovery, and ensuring that those who can undertake employment in ordinary industry are placed in suitable jobs. The first of these is met to some extent by the special arrangements made at seven of the Remploy factories and by the village settlements which have been established by voluntary organisations and local authorities. As regards the second problem, medical opinion holds that there need be no bar on the placing in ordinary industry of persons with certain types of infectious tuberculosis provided the employment is approved by the proper medical authority and the employer is informed of the nature of the disability.

Epileptics sometimes present a special problem because of the reluctance of some managements and fellow workers to accept them readily into employment. To counter this reluctance and encourage their employment in suitable work, a special leaflet has been prepared which describes the malady and explains how to deal with any fits which occur at work. The understanding and co-operation of employers and of the epileptic's fellow workers are essential if satisfactory resettlement is to be achieved. Experience does not suggest that epileptics should be segregated from their fellow workers. Although some misunderstanding persists, steady progress is being made in dealing with the problem, and the percentage of epileptics unemployed is not markedly higher than that for other classes of disabled.

The industrial rehabilitation and resettlement into work of the disabled is one of the most human problems with which the Ministry deals. The work certainly calls for the use of new and improved techniques both in the day-to-day 'case-work' and in the endeavour to perfect administrative arrangements to ensure that there is effective continuity in action throughout. From the commencement of recovery to absorption in the community the disabled person will be concerned with hospital and other doctors, social workers, voluntary organisations, local authorities, and other Government Departments besides the Ministry. Each must know the other's function and be ready to take up the responsibility at the appropriate time. A Committee of Inquiry under the chairmanship of Lord Piercy has lately reviewed the whole subject of the industrial rehabilitation, training and resettlement of the disabled and although it made a number of recommendations for changes and improvements, it was impressed by the completeness of the statutory provision which now exists for the service of the disabled and by the comprehensive and well-established facilities for enabling them to get suitable employment.

In the planning and development of employment services for the disabled it can fairly be claimed that Great Britain has led the world and visitors come from many different countries to study the working of the British system.

CHAPTER VI

Training for Employment

*

IN opening the debate on the White Paper on Full Employment in June, 1944, Mr Ernest Bevin said: 'An expanding economy entails a certain degree of mobility of labour as well as of industry. One of the first things we must do is to establish training under government auspices and no longer regard it as remedial action for long-term unemployment: it must be part and parcel of our economic system.' In addition to providing for the better distribution of labour by fitting workers from declining industries for jobs in expanding industries, training provides for the more efficient use of manpower through improvement in its quality.

Until 1944, apart from emergency legislation for resettlement purposes after the First World War and for subsequent war-time needs, the Ministry derived its authority to provide vocational training mainly from the Unemployment Insurance Acts; in normal times, therefore, training was restricted to unemployed persons. This legislative basis was altered by the Disabled Persons (Employment) Act, 1944, and the Employment and Training Act, 1948.

In practice, the Ministry has always accepted as a first principle that the primary responsibility for training workers must rest with the employer. Government training is intended to be only supplementary in order to meet national needs, and is invariably related to the capacity of industry to absorb the workers trained. The grounds for affording such training may be humanitarian, economic, related to special needs such as the defence programme, or a mixture of all three. In deciding policy as to new schemes of training both sides of industry are consulted, initially through the Joint Consultative Committee and later through the appropriate employers' associations and trade unions. During such discussions, the arguments for training by the exceptional method of a government training scheme at government cost are carefully considered and alternatives examined.

Training is mainly for skilled work and usually lasts six months or more. It is intensive, being the equivalent of roughly three years' ordinary apprenticeship in industry, and is organised on the basis of a standard five-day working week of $42\frac{1}{2}$ hours. Sometimes the special nature of training needed, the small number of applicants for the particular type of training, or the fact that facilities are already available make it preferable to arrange for the training to be given in technical or commercial colleges or at employers' establishments rather than at Government Training Centres. The arrangements whereby the training of severely disabled persons in some of the residential centres run by voluntary bodies is grant-aided by the Ministry have been described in the previous chapter.

Training Courses

As government training has to be related to the varying needs of particular sections of the community and to the capacity of industry to absorb the trained workers, the facilities provided are constantly changing. In extent, training has ranged from 32,000 places provided in Government Training Centres at the peak period in 1947 to slightly less than 3,000[1] in each of the last few years. In type it has varied from general reconditioning courses to highly specialised trade ones, and from the traditional crafts of the blacksmith and the carpenter to the developing ones of the precision instrument maker and the television mechanic. A brief description of the service in its four main periods will illustrate its potentialities and flexibility.

Between the Wars

It was as part of its general responsibility for the resettlement of ex-Servicemen disabled in the First World War that the Ministry, working in close co-operation with the Ministry of Pensions, entered the training field. Five of the instructional factories which the Ministry of Munitions had set up during the war were taken over to provide training in conditions similar to those in an ordinary production factory, but in a more intensive form than the ordinary workshop could afford to give. Between 1919 and 1924 the number of men thus trained was about 82,000. When these training schemes came to an end facilities were needed to train young men who, in this period of heavy unemployment, had had no opportunity of learning a trade and, in some cases, had never even had a job. This was the main task of the vocational training service from 1924 to 1938 and it is significant that even in those years 75 per cent of the 100,000 men trained were successfully placed in employment.

The Second World War

When preparations for the Second World War began, all training schemes not of direct value to the war effort were terminated, and training in the 16 Government Training Centres then in operation

[1] In the early summer of 1959 there were roughly 2,000 trainees in the Government Training Centres and another 1,000 in Residential Colleges for the more seriously disabled and in Technical Colleges, etc.

was concentrated on the engineering and allied trades in order to increase the labour force of the munitions industry. The majority of war-time courses were given in fitting, instrument making, machine operating, motor vehicle maintenance, sheet metal working, welding, draughtsmanship, electrical fitting, armature winding and electrical instrument repair. Although some women were recruited for training in 1939, it was not until 1940 that the limitation of training to those unemployed was removed and their recruitment, mainly for engineering occupations, was developed. In all, more than 525,000 men and women were admitted to courses of government training during the war period, when the number of Government Training Centres rose to 38 at the peak.

Towards the end of 1941 a review undertaken by the Ministry led to modifications in the length and type of training. Flexibility became the keynote. Special classes were set up where necessary to meet the needs of particular employers or industries; during the final period of training the instruction of individual trainees was frequently adapted to meet the practices of their employers.

The soundness of the new policy was well tested during the ensuing war years. Frequently, government training had to meet both bulk and individual demands for additional skilled workers at short notice. In 1942, to meet the need for riveters in the ship-building industry, a shipyard site was acquired at Glasgow and a training course established there which helped to make good the deficiency; later, on the same site, a course for electrical welders contributed towards closing a dangerous gap in labour supply. When the Chief Inspector of Factories was given power to require employers to provide canteen facilities for their workers, the Ministry arranged courses in canteen management and canteen cooking to fill consequential labour demands for canteen manageresses and cooks. The requirements of some individual firms were met, from 1942 onward, by training women with good educational qualifications and technical ability in specially designed courses in draughtsmanship, electrical fitting and inspection work; and some of these trainees were given a further background course in engineering principles and workshop practice to fit them to be assistants to planning and production engineers. Higher-grade training in occupational skills was instituted to assist employers who wished to up-grade their own workers but could not give the additional training themselves; these employers continued to pay their workers who were under training and the Government paid the cost of the training. To help to meet another pressing need part-time courses were organised to enable experienced workers to progress to foreman or charge-hand. From 1941 to the end of the war over 12,000 persons completed such courses which were generally conducted in technical colleges outside working hours. Similarly part-time training arrangements were made from 1943 for women shop supervisors and for employers and workpeople interested in production planning. Almost 600 women completed a course of the first kind and over 5,500 persons one of the second kind.

Towards the end of the war, with the falling-off in demands for labour by the munitions industries, training in the engineering trades was drastically cut, and the number of Government Training Centres was progressively reduced to 17. Courses in coalmining, which had been introduced in 1943, were expanded and plans were made on a twofold basis for post-war training. It was realised that training courses would be needed to meet the labour needs of basic and export industries and that government training would have to play an important part in post-war resettlement schemes for ex-Servicemen and women and for civilian war workers.

Post-War Resettlement Period

The same policy of flexibility and specialisation was pursued under the post-war training scheme which was launched in 1945. Training in the building crafts was the main item in this post-war scheme, and 33 specially designed Government Training Centres were built in order to deal with the large numbers of building trade trainees. These training centres, together with a number of emergency training centres that were opened in the immediate post-war years, raised the total number of centres to over 80. In all, courses in about 140 skilled occupations were organised in the early post-war years. Special needs were generously met; for example, a Government Training Centre was set up for the purpose of training operatives for the cotton spinning industry, which had been hard hit by concentration schemes during the war and which needed a great increase in skilled workers for its export drive.

The depleted labour force in the building industry had to be restored quickly in order to enable urgent repair and construction work to be put in hand. The scheme agreed with employers' and workers' associations, and operated in co-operation with 208 local advisory committees, provided for a period of six months' intensive training in Government Training Centres followed by a period of 14 months' further training and experience in the industry. Training was provided for all the main building craftsmen—including bricklayers, stone-masons, carpenters and joiners, painters, plasterers, plumbers, slaters and tilers. Training on building sites was carried out during the last two months of the six months' intensive course in many parts of the country. The Ministry, under contract with firms and local authorities, undertook building work with trainee labour. During 1947 trainees assisted in the construction of 1,800 houses, 21 blocks of flats and seven factories, while other work carried out by trainees included the decoration and repair of government property. In all, more than 50,000 building trainees have completed courses and entered the industry under this scheme, most of them in the immediate post-war years.

Training for agriculture, horticulture and forestry was arranged in consultation with the Ministry of Agriculture and Fisheries, the Department of Agriculture for Scotland and the Forestry Commission. The Ministry undertook to recruit trainees and determine their eligibility, while the other Departments accepted responsibility for assessing suitability and making the training arrangements.

As stated in the previous chapter, training in some occupations was reserved for disabled men and women, among whom priority was given to ex-Service applicants. The disabled were also given preference in allocation to other training courses, and among the able-bodied those who had served in the Forces took precedence over civilian war workers.

The completion of demobilisation, some falling-off in the heavy immediate post-war demand for skilled labour, and continuing full employment conditions (which enabled industry to absorb many workers without their being first given a course of training) led to a substantial reduction in the need for government training courses, and by early 1951 post-war resettlement requirements had been met and training places in Government Training Centres had been reduced to about 4,000. In some trades the need for training came to an end and the running of courses under a number of agreed schemes was suspended. Between mid-1945 and December, 1950, more than 132,000 men and women had completed government training courses.

Post-Resettlement Period

Since 1951 training efforts have been largely concentrated upon the requirements of the disabled and the ex-regular Serviceman. In addition to the permanent scheme of vocational training for the disabled, a scheme was introduced in 1950 for men and women completing a regular engagement in H.M. Forces as part of the plan to integrate Service and civilian life. The scheme offers a wide choice of trades to ex-regular Servicemen who need training to settle in suitable civilian employment. In addition to full-length courses for skilled work, in which men are trained to a high degree of skill, provision is made for refresher and conversion courses. Some craftsmen lose touch with their trade, perhaps through promotion, during their period of Regular Service, and the refresher courses are planned for them. Other men who have learnt a trade in the Services find it does not match the craft requirements of civilian life, and the conversion courses are designed to fit them for fully skilled civilian jobs.

In the immediate future, training activities will probably continue to be directed mainly to providing for these two categories. Should the necessity arise, however, a well-tested and flexible organisation is available to facilitate the deployment of workers whose skills may have to be adapted, or who may have to be retrained to meet new needs arising from changes in the balance of our industrial economy or the development of new techniques.

Administrative Arrangements

Applications for training may be made at any Employment Exchange and advice on the selection of a training trade is available at these offices. Disabled men and women apply through the disablement resettlement officer and a course of vocational training is recommended as the most satisfactory way to resettlement for a proportion of the men and women who complete courses at industrial rehabilitation units. The facilities available are made known to Regular Servicemen well before date of discharge through their Resettlement Interview Boards, on which the Ministry is usually represented. Great care is taken to ensure that those applying are suitable for the trade in which they seek training. They have to meet the standards of suitability set in agreement with representatives of the trade concerned and in some cases entry tests have to be passed. For a number of trades personal interviews with representatives of employers and workers are arranged.

Courses vary in length according to the complexity of the trade. In some crafts an initial government centre course is followed by continued training with a selected employer who normally receives a training fee. Each agreed training scheme is kept under review. Regional officers of the Ministry are in frequent touch with local representatives of the industries concerned and have the benefit of their advice and help on various aspects of the training schemes. This continuing consultation, together with regular analyses of the employment placing results and of the general labour situation area by area, provides a guide for the adjustment of the training facilities according to the industrial demand for trainees.

Government Training Centres are organised on the lines of a modern factory so that trainees are at all times working as nearly as possible under the conditions they will meet in industry. They are

G

grouped in classes of between eight and sixteen, depending on the trade taught, under a skilled instructor with considerable industrial experience. Progress is assessed by periodical tests throughout the course.

Newly engaged instructors are given an intensive initial course in the technique of instructing and from time to time receive refresher courses. Instruction in the centres is given by practice exercises interspersed each day with short informal talks on the shop floor. Formal lectures and instruction in theoretical principles are also given, their frequency and importance depending on the nature of the trade. Beginners are introduced to simple operations on training material and then, as the training course develops, have production work allocated to them. Experience has shown that this makes the training more realistic and stimulates the interest of the trainee. Where training is given at an employer's establishment, the employer is expected to conform to an agreed scheme of training. Similarly, the syllabuses followed at technical colleges and at residential centres are approved by the Ministry and generally follow the same lines as those in operation in Government Training Centres.

Except for cases where the training employer pays wages, all trainees are paid weekly maintenance allowances which vary according to age, sex and domestic responsibilities. There are special rates for those who live in lodgings away from home while training. Daily travelling expenses may be paid to able-bodied trainees with a long journey and are paid to all disabled trainees. No deductions are made from any of those payments for income tax or national insurance. Where it is normal in the trade for which a man has been trained for craftsmen to possess their own tools, a free tool kit is given to the trainee when he takes up employment in that trade.

Every effort is made to place trainees in their training trades, and although it is not possible to guarantee such employment to the individual trainee, the number of classes is regulated with this object in view. Placing action begins in the training centre office some four weeks before each trainee is due to complete his course; if a vacancy has not been found by the time the course is finished, placing action is continued by the local office nearest to the trainee's home under the supervision of the specialist training section at the regional office. Employers are encouraged to pay visits to their nearest Government Training Centre in order to earmark likely candidates for vacancies. The result of these arrangements has been that in the post-war period over 90 per cent of trainees have been placed by the Ministry in their training trade. In 1956, over 94 per cent were so placed.

Trainees from Abroad

Assistance has been given in some cases to trainees from abroad. During the war, a scheme was introduced with the object of accelerating munitions production in India. Parties of Indians were sent to this country for training courses in engineering occupations lasting approximately six months. By the end of 1946, over 800 men had been trained in this way and had spent a further period on production work in selected employment in this country. Arrangements were also made for groups of young men from the West Indies to be trained in general precision fitting, machine and tool reconditioning, jig and tool fitting, and capstan setting and operating for subsequent employment in the munitions industry in this country.

In the post-war period further developments took place. In 1946, a scheme was introduced for the training as higher technicians of Indians of graduate level, who had usually had at least three years' experience in their profession in India. These trainees were placed in the establishments of firms of repute in this country with a view to becoming qualified to fill managerial and executive posts in India and thus contributing towards the improvement of technical and administrative standards in Indian industry. The cost of maintenance, travelling and, where necessary, training fees was borne by the Indian Government. In the same year a special further education and training scheme for men and women from the colonies was drawn up and administered jointly by the Ministry and the Colonial Office. The objects of the scheme were to assist the development of the colonies and to facilitate the resettlement in civilian life of men and women who came to the United Kingdom to assist in the war effort and whose intention was to return to their home country on release from war service. During 1947 and 1948, over 1,200 trainees were accepted under this scheme.

In 1948, special arrangements were made for a number of young Turkish steelworks foremen to receive practical training in five establishments for a four-month period, the costs being borne by the Turkish authorities. In 1952, over 100 artisans from the Gold Coast were awarded two-year scholarships for training in Great Britain and were placed in the Government Training Centres, at technical colleges and at employers' establishments. The majority of them obtained either their Intermediate or Final City and Guilds Certificates, and a few their Full Technological Certificates before returning home.

Other trainees accepted for training since 1952 have come from the Sudan, Kuwait, Jordan, the Windward Isles, Indonesia, Ceylon, India, Pakistan, and other countries, for periods varying from six months to three years and these trainees have undertaken courses in a variety of different trades. For those who are to be instructors or foremen on their return home, training has included a short course at the Ministry's Staff College at Letchworth for the training of instructors and a three weeks' course in the three techniques of supervision—job instruction, job relations and job methods.

Training of Supervisors

This chapter would be incomplete without some description of the practical help which the Ministry is prepared to give employers in training their supervisors in the techniques of supervision. The increase in engineering production during the war years created the need for the up-grading of skilled men to posts as foremen and chargehands. In 1941, arrangements were made for courses of lectures in foremanship to be given at various technical colleges. Meanwhile, as an additional measure, the Ministry sent a representative to the United States of America to study the method of training supervisors within industry on the premises of the employer. This has since become known as the 'Training Within Industry Scheme for Supervisors' or, more popularly, as 'T.W.I.'

Through its three programmes of 'Job Relations', 'Job Instruction' and 'Job Methods', the Training Within Industry Scheme aims at developing three important skills that are essential to efficient supervision. These are skill in promoting good working relationships; skill in instructing workers, in giving directions, and in imparting clear information; and skill in utilising manpower, equipment and materials to the fullest extent by improving working methods. The free service offered by the Ministry in this field has been widely accepted by industry, and it is acknowledged by industrial experts all over the world that T.W.I. can play an important part in increasing productivity. T.W.I. methods are also being effectively used in Government Departments, the Armed Forces, and in trade union organisations. Following on a recommendation made in 1956 in the report of the Industrial Safety Sub-Committee of the National Joint Advisory Council, a new T.W.I. scheme known as the Job Safety programme has recently been introduced with a view to developing skills in the prevention of industrial accidents.

Although each of the programmes is primarily intended for supervisors themselves, the general pattern of the service from its early days has been for T.W.I. Training Officers on the Ministry's staff first to give an appreciation of the scheme to *managements*, in order to make them fully aware of the content and purposes of the training programmes and to encourage them to support its introduction at all levels in their organisations. Selection of suitable staff within the organisations follows, and those selected are then trained by officers of the Ministry to present the training programmes to their colleagues in supervisory grades generally, the aim being to promote a well-planned scheme of application in each firm. Training is given by the discussion method in groups of up to 10 at a time. Where a firm, perhaps because of its size, cannot select a suitable person to train its supervisors the latter can be trained by the Ministry's T.W.I. Training Officers in composite groups made up of supervisors from several small firms.

A quarterly publication, *T.W.I. Topics*, was issued by the Ministry up to 1957 to users of T.W.I. programmes in this country. The issue of this publication has recently ceased and articles concerning T.W.I. now appear in *Target*, the monthly bulletin produced by the Central Office of Information. This provides for a wide circulation to industrial firms in all parts of the country about developments in the field of T.W.I.

Five Regional T.W.I. Associations have been set up by firms in Great Britain who have introduced T.W.I. methods in their own factories and who consider that it would be in the interest of industry if use of the method could be more widely developed, and the Ministry's officers assist these Associations in their work to encourage the development of good supervisory training.

Over 4,500 firms have so far introduced the T.W.I. scheme, and by the end of 1957 more than 296,000 supervisors had received training in job instruction, 227,000 in job relations, 83,000 in job methods and 1,100 in job safety. In addition, a considerable number of persons from overseas had been trained in this country and are now developing the scheme in their own countries.

Special training courses, provided originally for the Ministry's own instructional staff, have in recent years been provided at the Ministry's Staff College at Letchworth for the training of craft instructors and foremen from industry in the techniques of teaching. The course takes place under workshop conditions, and it provides instruction and practice both in demonstrating workshop skills and in giving trade talks and trade lectures. Over 11,000 instructors and foremen from industry have taken this course during the comparatively short time that it has been thrown open to them.

In 1953 a Committee was set up to review methods in operation for the training of supervisors in industrial establishments. In its report, issued in 1954, the Committee drew attention to the need for the improvement of existing arrangements (including the T.W.I. scheme); for promoting interest by senior management in supervisory training; and for better co-operation between industry and the various bodies providing training. The report has been well received by industry. The recommendations on T.W.I. have been accepted and are being implemented, and a number of interesting developments have taken place in industry, technical colleges and elsewhere as a result of the Committee's Report.

CHAPTER VII

National Service

*

EVENTS in the post-war period have made it necessary for the Government to continue to impose an obligation on young men in Great Britain to perform a period of National Service. In April, 1957, however, the Government announced that they had decided to aim at stabilising the Armed Forces on an all-Regular footing by the end of 1962, and to plan on the basis that there would be no further call-up under the National Service Acts after the end of 1960. This was accompanied by a warning that if voluntary recruitment failed to produce the numbers required the country would have to face the need for some limited form of compulsory service.[1]

The Minister's authority to require young men to undertake National Service is derived from the National Service Acts, 1948 to 1950, that of 1948 being a consolidating measure which repealed the 1939 to 1947 Acts. The period of National Service is at present two years' whole-time and a certain number of days of part-time service spread over a maximum of three and a half years, after which men become members of the Reserve Forces and as such are liable to be called up in the event of an emergency. During whole-time service, when the initial training period is over, men may be sent on active service and many National Servicemen have served in Korea, Malaya and Cyprus.

The Acts lay down the general principles governing registration, medical examination and enlistment, while Regulations, which the Acts empower the Minister to make, prescribe the procedures for them. Certain of the provisions may be extended or amended by Order in Council; for example, in 1953, the duration of the 1948 Act itself was extended for a further five years by an Order in Council. Financial sanction is provided to cover allowances to the men for travelling, subsistence and loss of earnings at the medical examination stage. Claims for marriage allowance, which are normally submitted prior to enlistment, are paid by the Service Departments, and National Service grants are payable in certain circumstances through the Ministry of Pensions and National

[1] 'Defence—Outline of Future Policy', Cmd. 124, April, 1957.

Insurance, whether the claimant is married or single, to cover such commitments as liability for dependants, rent, mortgage repayments and insurance premiums.

The Acts aim at equity of treatment of all classes of the community but also seek to ensure that there will be no undue hardship in any particular cases. There are statutory provisions for postponement of call-up on the grounds of exceptional hardship. While the Minister has no power to grant exemption from National Service, he can arrange administratively for deferment of service since he is not obliged to call up at any particular time a man who has been medically examined under the Acts.

Registration

The National Service Acts, 1948 to 1950, impose a general liability for service on all male British subjects ordinarily resident in Great Britain who have attained the age of 18 but are not yet 26, or 30 in the case of registered medical practitioners and dentists. In 1955, an amending Act provided for the extension of the upper age limit to 36 in the case of men absent from Great Britain for not less than 28 days in the last year of their liability. A very small number of categories of men, such as those in holy orders or regular ministers of any religious denomination, are excepted from the provisions of the Acts.

The procedure has been for the Ministry to prepare a programme of registrations based on the National Service requirements contained in the annual statement on Defence made in the form of a White Paper by the Minister of Defence and to publish this programme as far ahead as possible. If, as in 1948 and in 1956–57, the number of men in the call-up field during the year was substantially greater than the Service requirements the balance has been adjusted by postponing a registration and allowing the age of call-up to rise. If, as in 1952, the number was substantially less the age of call-up has been allowed to fall. During the closing years of National Service, registrations have been less frequent than in the past and the age at which men might normally expect to be called up has therefore risen.

Young men becoming liable under the Acts at 18 years of age are subject to registration from the age of 17 years 8 months. Normally, men born in a prescribed quarter of an annual age class are called upon to register on a date announced by the Minister. All men of the ages stated in the announcement who are liable must register. Questions of postponement, deferment or conscientious objection are considered *after* registration, and the only doubtful point that can be discussed beforehand is whether a man is, in fact, liable under the Acts. Most cases can be settled in the local offices but, if not, they are referred to the Ministry's Headquarters for decision.

To provide the best facilities for the public, registration is undertaken by all the Ministry's local offices. Registrations are normally on Saturday to avoid, as far as possible, loss of working time for the men and to enable the Ministry's local offices to use their ordinary complement of staff for this additional work.

On registration, men are required to state their National Insurance number and to give certain particulars including details of their occupation. They are asked if they wish to express a preference for a particular Service. The information obtained from each man is entered on an individual record form which becomes a permanent 'control' document and on which all action is recorded until his final posting to the Services. On the Monday following registration the local offices, having classified each record with the appropriate occupational details, send the registration documents to the appropriate Regional Allocation Office at which the subsequent detailed work is done.

Deferment of Call-up

Deferment, which is discretionary, differs fundamentally from postponement, which is statutory. Postponement is related solely to a man's personal circumstances. The basic principle underlying deferment is that it should be granted only if, in its broadest sense, it would be in the national interest to do so: the individual deferment of apprentices, for example, in the interests of building up a skilled population; or the block deferment of men in certain vital industries. The Minister exercises administrative discretion in granting deferment in accordance with current government policy, and is thus able to ensure flexibility in meeting the changing needs of the nation.[1]

At the present time block deferment is limited to men in certain occupations in coalmining, certain groups in agriculture and one or two other very small but important categories. Fishermen who are members of the Royal Naval Reserve (Patrol) Service and members of the Merchant Navy are not called up since they are already where they would be needed as trained men if an emergency were to arise. Except for certain of those in the agricultural categories, no application for deferment need be made by the individual men. Where applications are necessary from those in agricultural

[1] The principle of deferment was first outlined in a White Paper (Cmd. 6831) issued in June, 1946.

employment, they are dealt with by National Service Deferment Boards advised by Panels, representative of both sides of the industry, appointed by County Agricultural Committees. A check is made initially to confirm that the deferred men are in the occupational categories covered by these deferment arrangements; further checks are made at intervals during the period of liability for service to ensure that they remain in these categories.

The initial application for individual deferment is normally made at the time of registration. A comprehensive system of peace-time individual deferment has now been built up to cover full-time students, apprentices, trainee technicians, learners in a similar position to apprentices, and pupils for the professions. Young men who wish to remain at school are granted deferment up to a maximum limit of the end of the school year in which they reach the age of 19. Students intending to take a full-time course for a university degree or a course of equivalent standard are granted deferment by University Joint Recruiting Boards. These Boards are composed of members of the University staff with a chairman nominated by the Vice-Chancellor of the University and appointed by the Minister. The secretary is an official of the Ministry. Deferment is at present granted for the length of time necessary to complete full-time studies to obtain degrees, for postgraduate research or for diplomas, but not beyond the upper age of liability; its continuance is subject to satisfactory progress.

All other individual applications for deferment are considered by National Service Deferment Boards. The Boards consider applications from apprentices and others in a position similar to apprentices, young men in training as technicians, articled clerks, and those attending certain full-time technical classes. They have to decide, among other things, whether a genuine apprenticeship or learnership of a type recognised by the industry or customary to the trade exists, or in industries and occupations for which there are no generally recognised or customary training arrangements, whether the training given by individual employers is of equivalent standard and will produce fully skilled men. They must also decide in the case of trainee technicians or men training for professional qualifications, whether suitable practical training in employment, or under articles combined with appropriate part-time studies, is being undertaken. The Boards also consider applications from men who, although unable to satisfy the practical training requirements of professional bodies, are taking part-time courses of study for examinations which are not below the Higher National Certificate standard. In addition, the Boards deal with cases of certain ex-apprentices employed in a few highly skilled occupations on a narrow range of 'priority' projects who may be granted post-apprenticeship deferment for a period of two years.

When a man's deferment is nearing expiry, his registration documents are sent to the Regional Allocation Office and medical examination is usually arranged six to eight weeks before the date of expiry so that there need be no delay in call-up; if the man is medically unfit for service in the Forces he is free to make his own arrangements to follow the end of his course of training.

Conscientious Objection

The arrangements for dealing with conscientious objectors introduced by the Military Training Act of 1939 have proved generally acceptable both in war and in peace and have been little changed by subsequent legislation.

The claim to conscientious objection is usually made at the initial registration but will be accepted until not later than two days after medical examination. The local office registers the man provisionally as a conscientious objector, gives him a form to apply to the Local Tribunal for Conscientious Objectors for inclusion in the Register of Conscientious Objectors and then sends his registration documents to the regional office, which is responsible for all further action. The application may be based on conscientious objection to being registered in the military service register, to performing military service or to performing combatant duties. Provision is made also for 'unconditional registration' in the extreme case in which a man is able to prove that he 'feels it is his duty to do nothing even to aid or comfort those engaged in military operations'.

The main administrative problems are to provide a method of testing the sincerity of the objection which is perceptive and impartial enough to satisfy both the conscientious objector and those who are called up for military service; and (except in cases of unconditional registration) to determine conditions which will relate the position of the conscientious objector as closely as possible to that of the man in the Forces. The National Service Act, 1948, provides that in appointing members of Local Tribunals to hear these cases 'the Minister shall have regard to the necessity of selecting impartial persons'. There are now five of these Tribunals in England, one in Scotland and one in Wales; each consists of a Chairman and six other members but only four of the ordinary members attend any one session. The Chairman in England and Wales is usually a County Court Judge, and in Scotland a Sheriff or a Sheriff Substitute.

The Tribunal may order the man to be placed on the Register with conditions, or without conditions, or as a person liable to be called up for non-combatant duties only. Those registered without conditions have no obligation under the National Service Acts. If, as is more frequent, a man is registered conditionally he is required to undertake civilian work, specified by the Tribunal, for a period corresponding as far as possible to the full number of days he would otherwise be required to serve in the Forces. Men registered for non-combatant duties are posted to the Non-Combatant Corps; the Service authorities have a statutory responsibility for seeing that they are employed only in non-combatant duties. The Tribunal may also direct that a name shall be removed from the Register of Conscientious Objectors in which case the man will be called up for National Service in the normal way.

A man who is dissatisfied with the findings of the Local Tribunal has an unrestricted right of appeal to the Appellate Tribunal. The Minister also has the right of appeal to the Appellate Tribunal against the decisions of Local Tribunals though in practice he has very rarely exercised it. The Appellate Tribunal sits in three divisions—in London, Manchester and Edinburgh.

Medical Examination and Service Interviews

Medical examination and Service interviews take place in 48 Medical Board centres provided and staffed by the Ministry and under the administrative control of the Regional Allocation Offices. Each centre is served by one or more of the 78 Medical Boards formed from standing panels of general practitioners in the area. Appointments to the panels are made by the Minister on the recommendation of the Ministry of Health or the Department of Health for Scotland, whose Regional Medical Officers supervise the medical work of the Boards.[1] A code of instructions for the guidance of the Boards has been agreed between the Ministry and the Service Departments. Each Board must consist of not more than five and not less than three medical practitioners, one of whom acts as Chairman.

Shortly after registration, men who have not applied for deferment or who are not eligible for it are summoned for medical examination, the oldest first. They are advised in the notice summoning them to examination that if they are suffering from disabilities which might affect their fitness for service they should bring with them medical evidence from their own doctor. If, for any reason, a man's call-up is delayed for more than six months after medical examination, he is re-examined. The medical examination may include reference to a consultant, and in most areas includes radiography of the chest. At the time of medical examination each man is asked to provide

[1] The Boards also undertake the medical examination of volunteers (men and women) for regular service in the Army and the Royal Air Force.

certain information about his educational and industrial history and to undergo simple intelligence and aptitude tests.

There are two systems of medical classification. The first, which is known as the 'Pulheems'[1] system of medical classification, is a functional assessment of the individual in relation to the qualities required for various employments in the Forces. This classification is used by the Service Departments to allocate a man to duties within his physical capacity and functional ability. The second is that required by the National Service Acts, which provide that a man, after examination by the Medical Board, must be placed in one or other of the medical grades laid down in the Acts. On completion of the medical examination each man receives a grade card showing the National Service medical grade in which he has been placed—I, IIA, II, III or IV, as the case may be. Any man who wishes to appeal against the grading given may do so. Men in the categories I, IIA and II are subsequently called up. The National Service medical grading is only used until a man is called up, and his medical category thereafter is based on the Pulheems assessment.

After medical examination those graded as fit for service are interviewed by the Service interviewing officers. The men's own Service preferences are carefully considered, but the intakes of National Servicemen into the Royal Navy and the Royal Air Force are much smaller than the numbers of men expressing a preference for these Services. A substantial number of those wishing to serve in the Royal Navy or Royal Air Force have, therefore, to be rejected, and to serve in the Army. The Royal Navy interviewer, provided he does not reject a man, seeks to settle as early as possible the branch in which the man is to be trained. In the Royal Air Force the final selection for trade training is made during the period of recruit training. The Army interviewing officer discusses with the man any preference he may have for a choice of corps or unit, or for any particular employment in the Army, and records the choice on the man's Army qualification form; this form is sent to the War Office who notify his final allocation to the Ministry for posting. Where he has to be allocated to a corps or unit other than that of his choice an explanatory letter is sent to him with his enlistment notice. At the Service interview the advantages of a regular engagement, including the wider training opportunities and better pay rates, are explained to likely candidates.

Each Service has made a careful job analysis of the various trade

[1] Pulheems: P for physical capacity; U for upper limbs; L for locomotion; H for hearing; EE for eyesight; M for mental capacity; and S for emotional stability.

and fighting occupations and has developed an effective method of assessing their functional requirements and relating them to the Pulheems system of medical classification. Full particulars of men with trade, occupational or educational qualifications in which the Services are specially interested are obtained well in advance of their posting and the individual allocation of these men is arranged with the Service Departments.

On completion of medical examination, the Regional Allocation Office transfers the registration forms of men available for call-up to the regional office posting section for the final stage of posting the men to the appropriate Service.

Postponement of Call-up

At the time of his medical examination, a man may apply for post-ponement of his liability to be called up on the ground of 'exceptional hardship' arising from his domestic, business or other personal circumstances. To justify postponement, difficulties must be unduly severe or abnormal and must either require time for alternative domestic or business arrangements to be made or be such that alternative arrangements cannot reasonably be made.

Applications for postponement are first considered locally by an official of the Ministry. If he considers that an application satisfies the regulations laid down, this officer will grant a postponement certificate; if not, he will refer the case to a Military Service (Hardship) Committee for decision. There are forty-seven of these independent statutory Committees each consisting of a Chairman (usually, but not always, a lawyer) and two members, one selected from a panel representing employers and one from a panel representing employed persons. An applicant may appeal against the decision of the Hardship Committee if its decision is not unanimous or by leave of the Committee. The Minister also has the right to appeal against the decision of a Hardship Committee. The appeal is made to the Umpire, an appellate authority independent of the Ministry and appointed by the Crown who sits with two assessors appointed by the Minister to hear an appeal.

Postponement certificates may be issued for periods up to two years and may be renewed if necessary for up to one year at a time. The upper age of a man's liability for service is increased by the length of postponement granted.

Posting to the Services

The approved annual allocation of National Servicemen for each of the three Services is spread evenly over the year, and is broken down into weekly intakes for the Royal Navy and the Royal Air

Force, and fortnightly intakes for the Army. These weekly (or fortnightly) numbers may be adjusted by agreement between the Ministry and the Service Departments to meet fluctuations in the numbers of volunteers for regular service.

The men available for posting are of two main groups: those in the current age class and those of earlier age classes who have become available at the end of deferment. Tables showing what has happened to men who registered after 1946 are published half-yearly in the *Ministry of Labour Gazette*. The tables give, for a fixed date, the numbers of men in each age class who have been called up or have volunteered for service, the numbers medically unfit, and the numbers by various deferment groups whose call-up is still deferred.

The registers in the regional offices of men available for posting are subdivided into Service groups and each week (or each fortnight for Army allocations), the regional offices send to the Ministry's headquarters an analysis of the contents of the registers. The Ministry then issues instructions to each regional office to post a quota based on the Services' requirements and the number available for posting in the region and carefully regulated to maintain an age balance within each group throughout the country. Where there is no delay through deferment, postponement, the need to see a medical consultant or for any other reason, call-up comes at approximately the same age for all National Servicemen. An enlistment notice is issued after completion of medical examination, ordering the man to report for service not less than 14 days later. If a man asks, with a good reason, for early call-up, efforts are made to meet his wishes subject to a minimum age limit of $17\frac{1}{2}$ years. Call-up under 18 may be allowed to those who intend to proceed to a University when they complete their National Service and wish to fit in as well as possible with the commencing date of the University session and to those who advance other very good reasons. The call-up of those over 18 is also expedited, wherever possible, if for good reason special application is made. Those who may apply are those already registered or men who have reached the age of 18 and wish to register and be called up in advance of their age group.

Call-up of Men to the Forces, 1957–60

The introduction of the new defence policy mentioned in the first paragraph of this chapter required that special arrangements be made for call-up during the concluding years of National Service. It was estimated that the Armed Forces would need to call up less than half the number of fit men liable for service under the Act, and the problem was to effect this in an equitable manner. The Government considered various solutions involving selective service, but decided to maintain the principle of universal service. The method adopted[1] was to rely as far as practicable on men who had enjoyed deferment, supplemented by younger men from new registrations. By this means the Services would be assured not only of the necessary numbers of men but also of a reasonable balance between younger unskilled men and older men with technical or professional qualifications. To enable young men to plan their futures, the Government published advice to the effect that if men were born before or during the first half of 1939 they were likely to be called up, while if they were born during 1940 or the final quarter of 1939 they were unlikely to be called up.

Safeguarding Civil Interests

Since the introduction of compulsory military service in 1939, legislation has included safeguards against men losing their jobs because of their compulsory call-up. The effect of this legislation is to impose on a worker's former employer—defined as the employer who last employed him within the period of four weeks immediately preceding call-up—an obligation to reinstate him in the occupation in which he was last employed or in an occupation not less favourable, provided it is reasonable and practicable to do so. An application for reinstatement must be made in writing within a prescribed period after the end of the worker's military service.

Cases of alleged evasion of this obligation are considered by Reinstatement Committees of which there are 47 appointed by the Minister for the purpose. Each Committee consists of a Chairman and two members representing employers and workers. If a Reinstatement Committee decides that the employer has defaulted in his obligations, an Order may be made requiring the reinstatement of the applicant, or the payment of compensation, or both. Appeals from the decisions of Reinstatement Committees are made to the Umpire.

In addition, an employer who dismisses an employee solely or mainly by reason of his liability for whole-time service in the Forces is liable on conviction to a penalty and to be ordered to pay compensation for the loss suffered by the man concerned; and a man whose employment is terminated by reason of his liability for part-time service following completion of his whole-time service in the Forces can claim compensation for the loss of employment.

There is also legislation[2] to safeguard a National Serviceman while he is serving, and for a period thereafter, against remedies for debt, where default in payment is due to service; eviction of dependants

---

[1] 'Call-up of men to the Forces, 1957–60', Cmd. 175 of May, 1957.
[2] The Reserve and Auxiliary Forces (Protection of Civil Interests) Act, 1951.

from the family residence; eviction from business premises; forfeiture of superannuation rights; and forfeiture of Industrial Life Assurance and Friendly Society policies.

Screening of Reservists

The position of individual reservists is constantly changing as National Servicemen called up since 1949 and later complete their two years' full-time service and come on to the Reserve and then on to the extended Reserve created by the Navy, Army and Air Force Reserves Act of 1954. While it is feasible only within certain limits to sort out in advance broad categories of occupations or skill whose degree of importance in a war can be clearly defined, a balance must be sought and kept for this kind of manpower planning. The Ministry has therefore the continuing function of identifying those of the volunteers for service in the Auxiliary Forces in peace-time who, because of their special skill or qualifications, should not be mobilised in war-time except possibly in a special capacity. It has the day-to-day task of screening the reservists whom the Service Department might wish to recall in an emergency and, as the older reservists advance in age and skill, of re-screening them.

H

PART III

Industrial Relations and Welfare

CHAPTER VIII

Industrial Relations

*

THE Ministry (and before it the Labour Department of the Board of Trade) has dealt with industrial relations since its inception. This term has generally been understood to cover the relations which arise from the determination of wages and conditions of employment both by Statute and by voluntary negotiation. It also includes the promotion of constitutional machinery for settling trade disputes within an industry, and the prevention or settlement of disputes through conciliation and arbitration. In its widest sense, it covers the promotion of good human relations in industry. In its narrower sense—the sense in which it is more generally used in industry today—industrial relations is held to include the relations arising from collective bargaining, which is the normal method of settling wages and other terms and conditions of employment. In the principal industries this bargaining goes on almost continuously between the employers or the employers' associations, on the one side, and the trade unions on the other. In many industries there is machinery for conciliation and for reference to arbitration of disputes that cannot be settled by other means, complementary to the arrangements for reaching collective agreement. The traditional policy is that industry should be given the fullest encouragement to settle its own affairs, and that the State should take action only when there is no effective bargaining machinery in an industry or when negotiations through an industry's machinery have broken down; this general principle underlies all legislation in this sphere.

The system of collective bargaining rests on the effective organisation of both employers and workers. The growth of trade union organisation in the modern sense dates from the period following the repeal of the Combination Laws in 1824, and this growth in turn stimulated the development of employers' organisations. By the middle of the nineteenth century the unions' efforts to secure recognition by employers had made sufficient headway to make possible the establishment of agreed relationships between them and employers or employers' organisations. Thereafter the development of union-employer relationships tended to follow two distinct lines. Some unions were able to secure the agreement of employers to the establishment of joint machinery for dealing with disputes. For example, in some industries conciliation boards were set up by joint agreement for the purpose of resolving differences. At the same time agreements were being reached between unions and employers determining the wages and the conditions of employment of the workpeople concerned. This twofold development, whereby joint arrangements for dealing with disputes grew up simultaneously with the emergence of joint collective agreements on wages and conditions, was of great importance and a special feature of this country. Without the former, the latter could not ensure the smooth functioning of industrial relationships. Together, they have played a large part in ensuring that industrial relations in this country were established on a sound basis.

The latter half of the nineteenth century also saw much legislation in the industrial relations field, itself a recognition of the new organisations which were emerging. Under the Trade Union Act, 1871, trade unions were no longer illegal at common law and the removal of this disability led to a rapid growth of trade unionism. In 1891 a Royal Commission was set up 'to enquire into the relations between employers and workmen and to report whether legislation could be directed to remedy any faults disclosed'. In its Report the Royal Commission acknowledged the value of the negotiating machinery which had been established. It sought ways of helping industry to extend the practices of conciliation and arbitration and of solving certain difficulties without weakening the voluntary nature of the measures adopted. The recommendations of the Commission were embodied in the Conciliation Act of 1896 which gave the Government a statutory responsibility for encouraging the development of negotiating machinery. It also empowered the Government to inquire into the causes and circumstances of a dispute, to appoint a conciliator or board of conciliation and, on the application of both parties, to appoint an arbitrator. The processes of conciliation, arbitration and inquiry which are still the main features of government action in trade disputes were therefore all dealt with in this Act.

During the First World War, with the consent of the employers and the unions, a system of compulsory arbitration coupled with a virtual prohibition of strikes was instituted in the field of munitions work. In spite of these arrangements labour unrest developed to such an extent that, in 1916, the Government appointed a Committee under the chairmanship of Mr J. H. Whitley, Speaker of the House of Commons, to inquire into the relations between employers and workmen and to report whether any weaknesses disclosed could be remedied through legislation.

The Committee issued five Reports and recommended in them: the formation in well-organised industries of joint industrial councils;[1] the appointment of works committees representative of the management and the workers in individual establishments; the statutory regulation of wages in badly organised trades; the establishment of a permanent Court of Arbitration; and that the Minister should be authorised to hold inquiries regarding disputes. The Committee stressed, as an overriding consideration, 'the advisability of a continuance as far as possible of the present system whereby industries make their own agreements and settle their differences themselves'. All the recommendations were accepted in principle by the Government and the Minister of Labour was given the responsibility for putting them into effect. Some were embodied in the Trade Boards Act, 1918, and some in the Industrial Courts Act, 1919.

Arrangements Within Industry for the Avoidance and Settlement of Trade Disputes

The Whitley Committee had hoped that the larger and already well-organised industries would find a way of fitting into the scheme for joint industrial councils but many of them, such as the engineering and shipbuilding, the iron and steel and the cotton industries, preferred to keep their existing negotiating machinery unchanged. Between January, 1918, and December, 1921, 106 new joint bodies were established, but only 47 of them survived the general strike of 1926.

By 1939, in spite of setbacks, the idea of Whitleyism was soundly established. During the Second World War co-operation between employers' associations and trade unions greatly improved. The increased organisation of industry and other conditions arising out of the war gave an impetus to the setting up of voluntary negotiating machinery in fields not already covered. The process has continued since the war and today almost all the main industries have some form of joint negotiating machinery. The structure of such machinery varies considerably, not only among the industries which retained their existing arrangements but also among the joint industrial councils themselves. Some act almost entirely as negotiating bodies for the settlement of wages and conditions of employment and do

[1] The recommendation reads: 'the establishment for each industry of an organisation, representative of employers and workpeople, to have as its object the regular consideration of matters affecting the progress and well-being of the trade from the point of view of all those engaged in it, so far as this is consistent with the general interests of the community'.

not, as was originally intended, consider the general problems of the industry. At the other extreme there are two councils, those for the printing and the heating, ventilating and domestic engineering industries, which do not deal with wages questions at all because these are within the province of other negotiating machinery in existence before the Whitley Council was formed. Most industries have made arrangements either within their joint wage-negotiating machinery or by separate constitutional machinery for settling disputes and about 70 of them have made provision for arbitration in disputes which cannot be settled by agreement.

An example of the way in which the procedure for settling disputes works in an industry which has not set up a joint industrial council is to be found in the engineering industry. In this industry there are 39 unions linked together in the Confederation of Shipbuilding and Engineering Unions. Most of the larger employers are organised in local associations which are affiliated to the Engineering and Allied Employers' National Federation. The procedure in the industry, which is usually referred to as the 'York Agreement', provides that when a dispute arises in a factory, discussion takes place first of all at shop-level between the management and the workers, accompanied if necessary by their shop-steward. Failing agreement, a works' conference may be summoned at which a full-time official of the union concerned and a representative of the employers' association may be present. Reference higher is to 'Local Conference' between union and employers' association officials, and if agreement is still not reached, the final stage is reference to 'Central Conference' at York at which only national representatives are eligible to decide questions although local officials may be in attendance. The agreement between the parties provides that until this procedure is exhausted there shall be no stoppage of work. If agreement is not reached at Central Conference, the parties are free to act as they wish and, in some instances, the dispute may be referred to the Ministry for conciliation and, if necessary, arbitration. So far as wages and conditions of employment are concerned, these are negotiated nationally between the employers' national federation and the trade unions.

The arrangements for arbitration also vary considerably. Some industries have a standing national board of arbitration; for example the coalmining industry has appointed a National Reference Tribunal. This consists of three permanent members having no connection with the industry and nominated by the Master of the Rolls, together with four assessors without voting powers, two chosen from each side of the National Negotiating Committee. Many industries, although they have no standing arbitration machinery, provide in their constitution for calling in an umpire or arbitrator as the need arises and many of them consult the Ministry on the choice of arbitrator. Others prefer not to include arbitration machinery in their constitution but to use the facilities offered by the Ministry by virtue of the Conciliation Act, 1896, the Industrial Courts Act, 1919, and the Industrial Disputes Order, 1951.

Government Action for the Prevention and Settlement of Trade Disputes

The Ministry's part in promoting harmonious industrial relations and preventing or settling disputes falls upon the Industrial Relations Department. The Chief Industrial Commissioner, as head of the Department, advises on general policy and keeps a close watch on events throughout the country. Under him, a staff of conciliation officers is stationed at Headquarters and in the regional offices. There is a constant flow of information, both on general matters and on individual disputes, between the officers at headquarters, who are in touch with head offices of the trade unions and the employers' associations, and the regional industrial relations officers, who are able to keep themselves informed of any local threat of dispute or significant change of industrial relations.

Conciliation

The role of a conciliation officer is essentially that of a peacemaker. The action he takes varies according to the causes and circumstances of the particular disputes and the relation between the parties, and cannot be governed by a precise code of procedure. His work is easier to describe than to define. He is not concerned merely with the settlement of disputes as they arise; he is often able by his advice to prevent incipient disputes from coming to a head—an important side of his work which, because it is largely informal and unobtrusive, rarely comes to the notice of the public.

In the course of his duties the conciliation officer is engaged in ascertaining the nature and extent of differences as they arise, securing the operation of established negotiating machinery for their settlement when such machinery is available, initiating action under his own auspices where established machinery has failed or is not available, and finally, in appropriate cases, endeavouring to arrange for arbitration where settlement by negotiation proves impossible. He must acquire knowledge of the industrial structure in his region; inform himself of the principles which govern relations between managements and workers, between organised employers and trade unions, and between the State and industry; and be ready to observe and interpret these principles when taking action.

A conciliation officer must always bear in mind the Ministry's policy of maintaining and strengthening the voluntary collective system whereby industry regulates its own affairs through its own machinery. When a dispute arises between employers and work-people who are parties to such machinery or to a recognised procedure for the settlement of disputes, it is no part of the normal functions of the conciliation officer to intervene. It is, however, within his scope to encourage the parties to make proper use of their machinery and he may have the opportunity for suggesting ways in which the procedure can be improved. He often finds it desirable to keep in touch with the two sides informally during the progress of discussions. Once the recognised means of settlement have been exhausted he is free to act as in cases where no machinery or procedure is available.

Where there is no procedure available for dealing with a dispute the conciliation officer is guided in considering whether or not he should intervene by the nature of the approaches made to him; in any event the time of actual intervention and the method to be adopted are very important. He may simply try in the first place to bring about direct discussions between the parties and with this object he can often usefully act as an intermediary between them. He can then discuss the differences with representatives of each side and make suggestions to them with a view to clarifying the issues. In other cases it may be desirable to arrange a joint conference over which he himself will preside, not as an arbitrator, but to help the parties to reach an agreement. He must work out his own techniques as no two disputes are alike, and the personalities involved and the relations between the representatives of the two sides often play a major part in the development of the situation. It must be stressed that whilst a conciliation officer will give all possible help in bringing about a settlement, any agreement reached is between the parties to the dispute and they must accept the full responsibility for it.

The work of the conciliation officer may be illustrated by an example. Having installed an expensive machine, a cotton firm sought the agreement of the trade union concerned to the introduction of two-shift working. This was refused by the union and the firm sought the assistance of the conciliation officer. A meeting was held under his chairmanship, at which there was a full discussion; following this the firm offered certain assurances to meet the trade union objections. The union again rejected the proposal and the firm sought further assistance from the conciliation officer. The matter was the subject of several private discussions with the parties over a period, as a result of which the stage was finally reached where the conciliation officer was able to arrange a meeting between representatives of the firm, the union and the workers directly concerned, at which he took the chair. The meeting provided the representatives of the firm with an opportunity to explain why they considered two-shift working was essential to secure the full use of the new machine, and the benefits which they expected to accrue both to the firm and their employees as a result. Following this statement the representatives of the firm and the conciliation officer withdrew from the meeting and the trade union officials and the workers considered the statement which had been made. Subsequently, on receipt of written assurances from the firm designed to meet the workers' fears of redundancies, the union agreed to the introduction of two-shift working on the new machine.

Voluntary Arbitration

When it is clear that a final settlement in a dispute cannot be reached through his efforts, the conciliation officer usually tries to persuade the parties to apply for the reference of the case to one of the forms of voluntary arbitration. If he is successful, he obtains a joint statement from the parties setting out the desired terms of reference and stating the form of arbitration required. All arrangements for arbitration are made at the headquarters of the Ministry.

The precise form of arbitration depends on the nature of the dispute and the wishes of the parties. The Conciliation Act, 1896, and the Industrial Courts Act, 1919, provide for arbitration by consent of both parties. Both Acts allow considerable flexibility with regard to the form of arbitration but the Industrial Courts Act imposes on the Minister a statutory obligation to avoid reference to arbitration until there has been failure to obtain a settlement by means of agreed arrangements existing in the industry concerned. The Minister may refer a dispute to the Industrial Court, or to a person appointed by him to act as a single arbitrator or as an independent Chairman, or to a Board of Arbitration. Arbitration awards under these arrangements are not legally binding on the parties concerned, but since they are the results of joint application they are almost invariably accepted.

The Industrial Court is a permanent and independent tribunal, although not part of the judicial system, and is not in any way subject to state or governmental control or influence. It does not replace forms of arbitration existing within industry itself, but it provides the continuity of experience often needed in disputes involving differences of principle or affecting whole industries. The Court consists of a President and two members, one of whom is a representative of employers and the other a representative of workpeople. In practice, most cases are decided by the President sitting with the same two members who are available on a full-time basis for the service of the Court, but panels of independent members and of members representing employers and workpeople are maintained by the Minister. These members act when any of the permanent members are unable to attend. All appointments to the Court are made by the Minister.

For the settlement of small local disputes the parties usually prefer a single arbitrator appointed by the Minister. Those chosen are often barristers, solicitors or university professors, who are appointed because of their knowledge of industrial relations matters. The arbitrator can have the assistance of assessors, but the assessors are not formally associated with the award and the extent of their activities is a matter for the arbitrator to decide. Reference to a Board of Arbitration is much less frequent. Membership consists of an equal number of representatives nominated by the employers and workers concerned and the Chairman is an independent person appointed by the Minister.

Compulsory Arbitration

The Acts of 1896 and 1919 do not provide means for compelling an unwilling party to go to arbitration. If the parties to a dispute have been unable to agree to go to arbitration, the procedure of the Industrial Disputes Order, 1951,[1] may be used at the instance of the party which seeks arbitration, without the agreement of the other party. This Order is an experimental modification of the policy introduced during the 1939–45 war, based on emergency legislation, that it will be reviewed whenever either side of industry so requests. The Order in operation during the war prohibited strikes and lock-outs pending action by the Minister and, in place of the long established right which it suspended, provided statutory access to speedy arbitration even though one of the disputing parties might not desire it.

The 1951 Order withdrew the prohibition of strikes and lock-outs but retained the system of arbitration at the instance of only one party as far as disputes on wages and conditions of employment were concerned. At the same time, in order to encourage and strengthen voluntary negotiating machinery, the right to invoke the Order was restricted to the parties to such machinery where it exists. Where there is no such machinery the use of the Order, apart from individual employers, is restricted to those organisations or

[1] The Industrial Disputes Order, 1951, was revoked in December, 1958. Later, a subsidiary feature of the Order, relating to the observance of industrial agreements, became part of permanent law in the spring of 1959 (Section 8 of the Terms and Conditions of Employment Act, 1959).

trade unions which represent a substantial proportion of employers or workers in the industry or section of industry concerned.

When a dispute is reported in this way, the Minister considers whether there is suitable joint machinery for the settlement of the dispute which has not been exhausted, and if so he is bound to refer the dispute to that machinery. If the dispute has already been the subject of an agreement, decision or award arrived at through joint machinery, or under the Conciliation Act or Industrial Courts Act, that agreement, decision or award must be treated as a final settlement of the dispute. The Minister may also take steps to promote a settlement by other means such as conciliation. If none of these considerations apply he must refer the matter to the Industrial Disputes Tribunal and most reports are in fact referred to the Tribunal. If the Minister considers that some form of coercive action, such as a strike or lock-out, is being taken by either party in connection with the dispute he may delay reference to the Tribunal; or, if he has already referred the dispute, he may notify the Tribunal that such coercive action is taking place and all proceedings will then be suspended until the Minister cancels the notification.

The Tribunal consists of five members; three, including the Chairman, are drawn from a panel of independent members appointed by the Minister and one each from panels of employers' and workers' representatives appointed by the Minister after consultation with the British Employers' Confederation and the Trades Union Congress respectively. The Tribunal is completely independent of government influence. Its awards are legally enforceable.

The cost of the Industrial Court and of the Industrial Disputes Tribunal and the expenses of single arbitrators and Boards of Arbitration are borne by the Exchequer. No charge is made to industry for arbitration under the auspices of the Ministry, but the parties have to bear their own expenses as well as the cost of verbatim shorthand notes if these are specially ordered by either party. Individuals appointed on a full-time basis to any of the statutory arbitration bodies are paid an annual salary; those appointed on an *ad hoc* basis are entitled to fees on a recognised scale. The Industrial Court and the Industrial Disputes Tribunal have officers of the Ministry as their secretaries. In cases involving single arbitrators or Boards of Arbitration the Ministry may also provide a secretary. Whether representation by counsel or solicitors should be allowed rests within the discretion of the arbitration authority concerned, but if either side is to be legally represented it is the practice for the other side to be notified of the fact before the hearing.

All awards of the Industrial Disputes Tribunal and the Industrial Court are published by H.M. Stationery Office. Awards of single arbitrators or of Boards of Arbitration appointed at the request of parties concerned are regarded as the property of the parties and their contents are not published or made available to others without the consent of the parties.

Inquiry and Investigation

Under the Industrial Courts Act, 1919, the Minister may, if he thinks fit, appoint a Court of Inquiry without obtaining the consent of the parties. This is normally done only in the case of disputes of national importance, and only when no agreed settlement seems possible and an unbiased and independent examination of the facts is clearly in the public interest. The Act requires that any report of a Court of Inquiry shall be laid before Parliament, thus providing a means of informing Parliament and the public of the facts and underlying causes of a dispute. The Court, consisting of an independent Chairman and equal numbers of employers and workers outside the industry concerned is not a standing body but is appointed by the Minister *ad hoc* and an officer of the Industrial Relations Department acts as its secretary. Although it is not the Court's function to act as an instrument of conciliation or arbitration and neither party to the dispute is bound to accept any of its recommendations, experience has proved that the impartial public examination of the facts has considerable value in the promotion of a settlement. The less formal method of inquiry available to the Minister under the Conciliation Act, 1896, enables him to appoint Committees of Investigation, usually constituted on the same lines as Courts of Inquiry. This procedure is used in cases where the public interest is less general.

The work done by the Industrial Relations Department in these various ways has been of great importance in bringing about better relations between employers and workers. The increase in the number of working days lost through strikes in the last few years, and the occurrence of some large and serious strikes, should not obscure the very real progress which has been made. In recent years there has been nothing to compare with the grave industrial unrest of periods such as that shortly before the First World War, or the turbulent decade of the 1920's. There are a number of reasons for this but the Ministry can fairly claim some share in the credit. This does not mean that either in the Ministry or outside there is room for complacency. Time lost through stoppages of work is always a waste and it is doubtful whether there has ever been a period in which this country could afford such loss. Today, when the national economy still maintains an uncertain balance, the consequences of stoppages of work can be, and often are, serious.

CHAPTER IX

Wages Boards and Councils

*

THE industrial relations work of the Ministry also includes the establishment of statutory Wages Boards and Councils and the enforcement by a Wages Inspectorate of statutory minimum remuneration fixed by them.

The regulation of wages and working conditions through collective agreement between both sides of industry can be effective only if the parties to the agreement are sufficiently strongly organised to ensure that its terms will, in general, be implemented. In some industries or trades it is not easy to build up a strong organisation; for example, those in which the workers are widely scattered, or work in small detached groups, or have to compete in an over-stocked or irregular labour market. In many of these the need has arisen for statutory wage-regulating machinery, but the Government welcomes and encourages the development of joint voluntary machinery within them in the hope that a stage will be reached when state intervention will no longer be needed.

The basis for such intervention has changed over the years. When the first Trade Boards Act was passed in 1909, its purpose was to ensure that a fair minimum wage would be paid to workers in the 'sweated' trades. Trade Boards had power to fix a statutory minimum wage which, when confirmed by a Minister of the Crown, could be enforced under the criminal law. An inspectorate was set up in the Board of Trade for the day-to-day administration and enforcement of the Act. The duties of the Board of Trade under the Act were transferred in 1917 to the newly created Ministry of Labour.

By 1939, when there were 51 Trade Boards, the original aim of mitigating under-payment in its worst form had come to be regarded as only secondary to the stimulus given by the system to the growth of organisation among employers and workers. It was hoped that this would lead eventually to the replacement of statutory wage regulation by voluntary collective bargaining.

During the Second World War statutory wage-fixing machinery was set up for the catering industry by the Catering Wages Act, 1943. This provides for a permanent Catering Wages Commission, whose functions are to investigate the need for statutory wage machinery in the various sections of the industry. The Commission has certain wider powers of inquiry and report beyond the field of wages machinery. Four Catering Wages Boards have been set up to cover the broad divisions of the industry.[1]

The Wages Councils Act, 1945, brought the policy of statutory wage regulation still closer to the Whitley ideal.[2] The Act substituted the term 'Wages Council' for 'Trade Board' to try to remove finally the conception that these existed solely or primarily in 'sweated' trades. Under this Act the Minister retained the power to set up a Wages Council, without formal inquiry except in case of objections, for any group of workers for whom there was no adequate wage-regulating machinery, if this was expedient 'having regard to the remuneration existing among the workers'. He was also given new powers designed to enable Wages Councils to be set up in industries where, though remuneration might not be unreasonably low, it seemed likely to become so because effective voluntary machinery either did not exist or seemed likely to cease to exist or to be adequate. The Minister may act on his own initiative in this, or the approach may come from a Joint Industrial Council. In either event the Minister refers the proposal to a Commission of Inquiry before making a Wages Council Order to establish a new Wages Council. Between 1945 and 1954, 10 new Wages Councils were set up in various retail and distributive trades, and in hairdressing. In most of these trades there had been Joint Industrial Councils which had found themselves unable to regulate remuneration effectively and which had therefore made application to the Minister for the establishment of Wages Councils. In addition the Rubber Proofed Garment Wages Council was set up in 1956.

The Act gave Wages Councils a wider field of operation than that of the Trade Boards. Whereas the latter covered workers in specific trades the *former* are related to workers employed in the *industry* including, for example, clerical workers. Wages Councils also have more extensive wage-fixing powers, for, whereas Trade Boards fixed minimum rates of *pay*, they fix minimum *remuneration* and this often

[1] The Catering Wages Act, 1943, was repealed as from 30th May, 1959, by the Terms and Conditions of Employment Act, 1959, which abolished the Catering Wages Commission and converted into Wages Councils the four Catering Wages Boards which were then functioning, i.e. (1) licensed residential establishments and licensed restaurants, (2) industrial and staff canteen undertakings, (3) unlicensed places of refreshment, (4) licensed non-residential establishments.

[2] The Whitley Committee (see Chapter I) had suggested that Trade Boards need not be restricted to 'sweated' trades, but should be extended to industries in which there was little or no organisation 'pending the development of such degree of organisation as would render feasible the establishment of a National or District Councils'.

includes payment for a guaranteed week; they may also fix holidays with pay for more than the one week permitted to the Boards. The Councils retain the powers possessed by Trade Boards to make recommendations to the Minister or to any Department about 'industrial conditions', and these have sometimes been used to good effect.

The Minister has power to abolish a Wages Council. Since 1947, five Wages Councils have been abolished—those in the furniture manufacturing, the tobacco, the rubber reclamation, the rubber manufacture and the hand-made chain trades. In the first four cases the Minister's action was taken in the light of a claim submitted by the industry that there was in existence a Joint Industrial Council or similar body capable of regulating wages and conditions; in the case of the chain trade, the Council had not met since 1939, and the wages had since been regulated by voluntary agreement. The Minister may also vary the scope of a Wages Council. Two such variations have been made since 1945—in the aerated waters industry in England and Wales and in the boot and shoe repairing trade.

In 1948, an amending Act was passed which converted the Road Haulage Central Wages Board into a Wages Council and made certain other amendments to the 1945 Act. The two Acts are now cited together as 'The Wages Councils Acts, 1945 to 1948'.[1]

The Composition and Procedure of Wages Boards and Councils
Membership consists of representatives of employers and workers in equal numbers, together with not more than three 'independent' members, one of whom is appointed to act as Chairman. All appointments are personal and are made by the Minister. The independent members are usually drawn from the legal profession, University professors and social workers, but the Minister may appoint any person he considers suitable. Representative members are, in the main, the nominees of the employers' or workers' organisation, but there are still some 'unorganised' employers and workers on Wages Councils. The object is to give representation as far as possible to all the main types of establishments and classes of work affected and the principal districts in which the workers are employed.

The statutory rates and conditions of employment framed by a Wages Board or Council are minima, and are not intended to discourage the payment of higher rates of wages or the observance of more favourable conditions of employment by arrangement between the employer and worker or under a collective agreement. On the other hand 'contracting out' is not permitted either to an employer or to a worker. To meet the problem of workers prevented by injury or infirmity from earning a minimum time-rate, who

---

[1] The Wages Councils Act, 1959, consolidated the various enactments relating to Wages Councils.

I

might find it difficult to obtain a job, a Board or Council may grant a permit authorising the employment of a worker in these circumstances at less than the statutory minimum remuneration.

All proposals for new regulations are announced in the London or Edinburgh *Gazette* or both, according to the field of operation of the Board or Council, and the Wages Boards or Councils also send a notice to every employer known to be affected. The employers are required to exhibit the notices, which specify a period within which employers or workpeople (and others) may make representations about the proposals to the Wages Board or Council. If the Board or Council then decides to go ahead with the proposals—with or without amendment in the light of the representations—it submits them to the Minister with the formal request that he should give effect to them in a Wages Regulation Order. The Minister must then either make an Order to give effect to them or refer the proposals back to the Wages Board or Council for reconsideration. The basic idea that the self-government of the industry should be maintained is underlined by the fact that the Minister has no power to vary the proposals.

The Wages Inspectorate

The Ministry's Office of Wages Boards and Councils sends copies of notices setting out the provisions of Wages Regulation Orders to all employers known to be affected by them. The employers are required to post three notices in a place where they can be read by the workers. They are also required to keep records of hours worked, piece-work operations completed, wages paid and holidays with pay allowed, sufficient to show whether or not they are complying with the Orders.

To secure a satisfactory standard of compliance with the Orders there is a Wages Inspectorate organised regionally under the general control of a branch of the Industrial Relations Department at Headquarters. Wages inspectors inquire into all allegations of non-compliance and also carry out a planned programme of routine inspection. They are vested with authority to enter at all reasonable times premises at which workers affected by a Wages Regulation Order are employed; to examine and take extracts from wages and other relevant records; and to question the employer and workers respecting compliance with requirements of the Acts and Orders.

The Acts empower Wages Inspectors to institute criminal proceedings in cases where offences seem to have been committed; as for example, where there is failure to allow a holiday with pay or where wages are less than the prescribed minimum. Subject to the Minister's general or special directions, the Inspectorate may also institute civil action on behalf of a worker for recovery of arrears of pay. In practice, however, the Inspectorate tries to secure compliance through advice and persuasion and resorts very infrequently to legal proceedings. During 1957, for example, only nine employers were prosecuted and civil proceedings were taken in one case only.

There are now 59 Wages Councils[1] and four Catering Wages Boards, covering over 500,000 establishments with about five and a half million workers. In three industries Wages Councils have recently been abolished and others may follow this example, but in many of the industries concerned organisation is not yet strong enough for such a development. It seems likely, therefore, that this system of partial collective bargaining, with statutory enforcement of the agreements reached, will continue for some further decades.

Baking Industry (Hours of Work) Act, 1954

The Wages Inspectorate is also responsible for the enforcement of the Baking Industry (Hours of Work) Act, which restricts night-work in the baking industry; it was passed in 1954 but did not come into force until 1st January, 1958, time having been allowed for bakery firms to undertake any necessary reorganisation. The Act was based on the unanimous Report presented in 1951 by a Committee, under the chairmanship of Sir Frederick Rees, which had been appointed in 1950 to consider the desirability of abolishing or

[1] There are Wages Councils in the following industries. (The asterisk denotes that there is a Council for Scotland separate from that for England and Wales.) *Aerated Waters; *Baking; Boot and Floor Polish; Boot and Shoe Repairing; Brush and Broom; Button Manufacturing; Coffin Furniture and Cerement Making; Corset; Cotton Waste Reclamation; Cutlery; *Dressmaking and Women's Light Clothing; Drift Nets Mending; Flax and Hemp; Fur; Fustian Cutting; General Waste Materials Reclamation; Hair, Bass and Fibre; Hairdressing Undertakings; *Hat, Cap and Millinery; Hollow-ware; Jute; Keg and Drum; Lace Finishing; Laundry; Linen and Cotton Handkerchief and Household and Linen Piece Goods; Made-up Textiles; *Milk Distributive; Ostrich and Fancy Feather and Artificial Flower; Paper Bag; Paper Box; Perambulator and Invalid Carriage; Pin, Hook and Eye and Snap Fastener; Ready-made and Wholesale Bespoke Tailoring; *Retail Bespoke Tailoring; Retail Bookselling and Stationery; *Retail Bread and Flour Confectionery Trade; Retail Drapery, Outfitting and Footwear; *Retail Food; Retail Furnishing and Allied Trades; *Retail Newsagency, Tobacco and Confectionery; Road Haulage; Rope, Twine and Net; Rubber Manufacturing; Rubber Proofed Garment-making Industry; Sack and Bag; Shirtmaking; Stamped or Pressed Metal-wares; Sugar Confectionery and Food Preserving; Tin-Box; Toy Manufacturing; Wholesale Mantle and Costume.

The Wages Council for the Drift Nets Mending industry is inactive, and has not met for several years.

By the Terms and Conditions of Employment Act, 1959, the four Catering Wages Boards then functioning were converted into Wages Councils. See footnote to page 128.

limiting the practice of night-baking. It provides, broadly, that every bakery shall choose either to employ no workers on bakery work between 10 p.m. and 5 a.m. (except on one night a week to meet week-end requirements, and in certain special circumstances) or to give notice of operation as a night-bakery, in which case no bakery worker may be employed between the hours of 6 p.m. and 6 a.m. for more than 26 weeks in the year or for more than four consecutive weeks at any one time. The Minister has power to exempt from the operation of the Act employers covered by a voluntary collective agreement regulating night-work, and two such exemption orders have been made, in respect of the National Working Agreement of the Scottish Baking Industry and of the National Agreement covering Co-operative Society bakeries in England and Wales.[1]

[1] A further exemption order was made in December, 1958, in respect of establishments covered by the national working agreement between the Federation of Wholesale and Multiple Bakers and the Amalgamated Union.

CHAPTER X

Human Relations in Industry

*

DURING and after the Second World War, all who were concerned with industry became increasingly aware of the importance of good relations between management and workers in the individual industrial unit, in the factory, pit or on the construction site. As early as 1917 the Whitley Committee had recognised the significance of these relationships and the concern which the State has shown for many years in the promotion and maintenance of good industrial relations has thus been extended to include the promotion of good human relations in industry. This has come about because today good relations between management and workers in the individual firm have come to be regarded not only as an end desirable in itself, but also as a matter of great importance from the standpoint of the national economy. On the one hand there is the social need to try to make man's work a satisfying and satisfactory part of his life and, on the other, the urgency of the call for increased production and productivity to safeguard the economic position of the country. The State recognises that the improvement of human relations in industry is a matter primarily for industry itself, but accepts that it has itself a duty to make the national needs widely known and appreciated and to provide assistance, as required, and particularly through advisory machinery and the furtherance of education and research.

Apart from a war-time Order relating to welfare,[1] there has been no statutory sanction for work in this field. The Ministry provides a Personnel Management Advisory Service whose function is to foster good human relations in industry. The service works in close co-operation with the voluntary bodies operating in this field of social and industrial welfare; these include the British Institute of Management, the Institute of Personnel Management, the Industrial Welfare Society, the British Association for Commercial and Industrial Education and the National Institute of Industrial Psychology.

[1] See Chapter VIII.

There has been growing recognition in industry in recent years that studies by social scientists and others can assist in the development of improved arrangements and techniques for reducing friction between management and workers and for solving or mitigating problems which arise in changing social and industrial conditions. The growth of such research by academic, industrial and voluntary organisations has been encouraged and assisted financially by the State. The Ministry, as a general rule, does not undertake or finance research in this field but maintains liaison with the Government Research Departments which, *inter alia*, make grants for research into human problems in industry. The Conditional Aid Scheme for the use of counterpart funds derived from economic aid given by the United States of America under the Mutual Security Act of 1952, enabled the State to sponsor an expanded programme of studies and research. A number of projects were directly financed by the Ministry from these funds.

The Whitley Committee recommended in 1917 that works committees representative of management and workers should be appointed in individual establishments. It expressed the view that 'a permanent improvement in the relations between employers and employed must be founded upon something other than a cash basis. What is wanted is that workpeople should have a greater opportunity of participating in the discussion about and adjustment of those parts of industry by which they are most affected.' The recommendation was re-stated by the Minister, Mr. Ernest Bevin, in 1940 and again by the National Joint Advisory Council in 1947. The Acts by which various industries were nationalised in the post-war years each contained a clause requiring the Board of the industry to consider with the trade unions concerned the need for the establishment of joint consultative machinery in the industry.

Except in a comparatively few firms pioneering in the field of good human relations in industry, joint consultation through works councils made comparatively little progress in the inter-war years. But some progress was made in another way. 'Labour management', which included in its scope the promotion of joint consultation, was gaining ground as a specialist function of management. The exigencies of war gave a great fillip to this trend. In July, 1940, the Minister, Mr Ernest Bevin, with his understanding of the part that the proper handling of human relations can play in human happiness and higher production, made the Factories (Medical and Welfare Services) Order. This empowered the Chief Inspector of Factories to direct certain factories to make satisfactory arrangements for the supervision of the welfare of their workpeople. There was, however, a great shortage of people with the appropriate training and experience to undertake this work. To remedy this, the Ministry, in co-operation with the Institute of Labour Management (now renamed Institute of Personnel Management), arranged a series of short intensive training courses in labour management both for new entrants to industry and for inexperienced officers already in it. The specialist officers after appointment were variously termed personnel officer, labour manager, welfare officer or staff manager, and sometimes the duties allotted to them were equally diverse.

In the post-war period it was felt by the Government and by many employers that the developments that had been secured in the field of personnel management should be maintained and extended. Accordingly, in 1945, the Ministry set up its Personnel Management Advisory Service functioning at first under its Factory Department and later under the Industrial Relations Department. A small staff of officers with industrial experience as personnel officers was recruited. Their duties were to give practical help and guidance to firms wishing to improve their personnel management, to the less experienced personnel officers in industry, and to the smaller firms without a specialist department. They co-operated with the professional and educational bodies in arranging lecture courses for personnel officers, tutoring these themselves where necessary. They took every opportunity of fostering joint consultation in industry both on the formal basis of works committees and through more informal arrangements for the interchange at all levels of ideas, views and information.

The advisers,[1] stationed at the Headquarters and in the regional offices of the Ministry, make over 2,000 visits each year by invitation or introduction, an average of 700 being new contacts. They are consulted not only on the setting-up of new personnel departments but also on a wide variety of aspects of personnel policy and practice. They do not attempt to give a detailed consultancy service—where appropriate they refer firms to the specialist organisations—but from their wide experience of personnel management and their collective observation of the causes of failure and success of various techniques in individual firms they are able to give guidance in particular cases and to indicate broad lines of application. The greater proportion of their visits are paid to the smaller and medium-sized firms but managements of larger organisations use them increasingly as a source of information on special questions and to discuss general developments in the field of human relations. They

[1] There were 17 Personnel Management Advisers in post in the Ministry at the end of 1957.

are consulted also by trade unions, employers' associations and the nationalised industries.

Progress in the work is steady. Many firms have come to realise that good personnel management is as important as good production and good sales management. The scope of the Personnel Department, as a service department to production, has widened and has come to be recognised as covering all matters affecting the morale and well-being of employees, individually and collectively. Thus it is concerned with recruitment, selection, training, education and promotion of staff and workpeople; the co-ordination of employee services; local negotiation and administration of industrial agreements relating to terms of employment, working conditions and wages; the promotion of joint consultation and works communications; and procedures for the avoidance of industrial disputes. Increasingly, directors have appreciated the need for laying down a sound personnel policy and appointing a member of the Board to be responsible for this policy. There has been a greater willingness on the part of firms to give their employees information on the trading and financial position of the firm and to see that effective communications are maintained at all levels. Many managements have begun to realise that the modern trend in firms towards amalgamation and centralisation of control tends to produce a feeling of remoteness, and consequently of apathy, in the individual worker unless this is effectively countered and his status and 'feeling of belonging' encouraged through effective means of consultation and communication.

Full employment with the consequent shortage of manpower has provided a spur to these developments; employers have been anxious to keep their workers, to avoid the loss of training costs involved in excessive turnover or poor selection, and have been conscious of the improvement in productivity which comes when men's energies are released through the incentive of having congenial and essential work and being members of an efficient and happy undertaking. The educational activities of the advisers have had to be adapted to this awakening interest. The arrangement of courses, conferences and discussion groups for senior management line executives and supervisory staff takes as much of their time now as do the courses planned for personnel officers. The awakening of interest was also evinced when, in 1952, the Ministry organised a national three-day conference on Human Relations in Industry. This was attended by over 400 delegates and observers from many parts of the country representing, as well as many individual firms, the British Employers' Confederation, the Trades Union Congress, the managements of Nationalised Industries, the principal institutes for the study of management and industrial welfare, Universities and colleges, medical societies and other voluntary bodies, and several Government Departments.

Although in many firms and industries the activities of the Joint Consultative Committees have become a real factor in the life of the organisation, elsewhere formal joint consultation has proved somewhat disappointing. Joint Production Committees were set up in many industries during the 1939–45 war and functioned successfully, but many were disbanded when war ended. After the action taken by the National Joint Advisory Council in 1947, there was a re-awakening of interest and works councils were established in many industries on the recommendation of employers' associations and trade unions. For a variety of reasons some of this interest has flagged although other, often more informal, methods have made steady progress. As technological changes are introduced into industry the need for consultation becomes increasingly necessary.

In this aspect of its work, the Ministry has undertaken varied and widespread publicity. In 1951, an exhibition showing good current practice in industry was staged for several months in the Industrial Health and Safety Centre. Following the 1952 conference, a report of its findings was published. In co-operation with the Central Office of Information the Ministry has also made available to industry three short films dealing with works information, the introduction of the new worker to his firm and job, and the advantages of supervisory training. A 'True Story' series of booklets, widely distributed, have as their themes joint consultation, works information and the selection of applicants for work. A still more liberal distribution was made, in 1954, of a leaflet summarising the recommendations of a Sub-Committee of the National Joint Advisory Council set up to examine the steps which could be taken to promote good human relations in industry.

There is little doubt that the efforts of both sides of industry, of good employers of the voluntary organisations concerned, and of the Ministry have resulted in a wider recognition of the value of, and need for, good human relations in industry. But progress is slow in relation to what is required in the changing industrial scene. For in industry the pace of development has recently quickened— in the techniques of production and in the application of atomic energy and of electronic controls. There is, too, a changing pattern in industrial organisation. Hence it is of great importance that, through real consultation between management and workers, the changes should be made smoothly and in a spirit of co-operation. Speaking of human relations, Sir Walter Monckton, then Minister of Labour and National Service, said:

'The introduction of any new method inevitably puts a strain on human relationships in an undertaking; they must be strong enough to stand the strain. And that strength is most easily found when there is in the minds of management and their workpeople that confidence in each others' good faith and integrity which is the basis, and the only basis, of good human relations in industry.'

CHAPTER XI

Safety, Health and Welfare in Industry

*

THE maintenance of adequate standards of safety, health and welfare in industry has been an objective of government policy since early in the nineteenth century when the first factory legislation was introduced and inspectors appointed to enforce it. The full significance of the important part these factors play in the supply of labour and its sufficient use, and in fostering industrial peace and good human relations, was not realised until the Second World War. It was in June, 1940, that the responsibility for the administration of the Factories Acts was transferred from the Home Secretary to the Minister of Labour and National Service. The transfer at that time was made necessary in order to ensure the close co-ordination of the work of promoting good working conditions inside the factories with the arrangements for regulating labour in war-time and for promoting the welfare of workpeople outside the factory, and generally securing goodwill in industry. When the transfer took place a Factory and Welfare Department was established in the Headquarters of the Ministry consisting of the Factory Inspectorate, an administrative section and the new 'outside' welfare service. With the end of the war, the work of the 'outside' welfare service greatly diminished, and the work in connection with safety, health and welfare is now carried out by a Safety, Health and Welfare Department consisting of an Administrative Department and the Factory Inspectorate.

Factory legislation constitutes a comprehensive code covering safety at work, the prevention of industrial disease, the hours of employment of women and young persons, as well as cleanliness, overcrowding, ventilation, heating, lighting, canteens, rest facilities, and the provision of first aid. The Factories Acts, 1937 and 1948, are the major legislative measures now extant.

The Ministry's policy is to obtain a continuing improvement in standards, both by the application of the Factories Acts and as a result of the voluntary efforts and co-operation of employers and workers and their organisations. Where standards are prescribed under the Acts, the main responsibility for maintaining them is placed on the employer, although certain responsibilities are also placed on the worker.

Safety

The 1937 Act, with the amending 1948 Act, while maintaining earlier basic safety requirements, added detailed clauses relating to particular matters, and stipulated that certain parts of new machinery sold or let on hire must be properly fenced by the maker. Safety requirements now concern the fencing of machinery; the safety of lifts and lifting appliances and tackle; protection from dangerous substances or circumstances; protection against explosions; the safety of workplaces and means of access to them; the training of young persons at dangerous machines; and means of escape in the event of fire. In addition, many Codes of Special Regulations contain safety requirements for particular industries; for example, for potteries, foundries, chemical works and works in which celluloid or cellulose solution is made or handled, while other Codes cover such non-factory employments as shipbuilding, docks and building operations.

Health

The requirements for industrial health aim at creating a good working environment by regulating such matters as cleanliness, temperature, ventilation and overcrowding and also at removing or minimising health hazards by the removal of harmful dusts and fumes from the working atmosphere. Factory doctors are appointed to examine young persons on entry into factory employment and annually thereafter until the age of 18 is reached. They also carry out investigations into cases of industrial disease. Special regulations are applied to impose particular requirements, for example regular medical examinations of workpeople, in industries for processes with a particular risk. Among such risks are those of lead poisoning, pneumoconiosis and anthrax. In the case of anthrax certain classes of wool and hair that are particularly liable to be infected must be disinfected immediately on import and before being sent to factories. This disinfection is carried out at the Government Wool Disinfecting Station, Liverpool, which is operated by the Ministry.[1]

[1] In 1957 a Committee of Inquiry was set up, with Mr R. F. Levy, Q.C., as Chairman, 'to consider the existing legal provisions concerning the importation of goods infected or likely to be infected with anthrax and the precautions to be taken in connection with such imported goods for the protection of the health of persons and to make recommendations'.

Welfare

Welfare, in its modern connotation, became the official concern of the Factory Inspectorate during the war of 1914–18. For emergency purposes it was necessary to legalise the employment of women and young persons in circumstances not permissible under the Acts, and various Emergency Orders had to be issued to meet the situation. In several of these Orders the provision of welfare facilities was made a condition of employment. Part of the Factories Act, 1937, dealt with welfare and included provisions as to the supply of drinking water, washing facilities, accommodation for clothing, seating facilities and first aid.

The period of the Second World War, like that of the first, saw a great extension of factory welfare. In June, 1940, the Minister appointed a Factory and Welfare Advisory Board to advise on welfare questions and to assist in developing and stimulating safety, health and welfare arrangements inside the factory, and lodging, feeding and other welfare arrangements outside the factory. At the same time a new Welfare Department was established in the Ministry, charged with the duty of developing welfare facilities for war workers outside the factories. A regional Welfare Officer was appointed for each of the Ministry's 11 Regions and Local Welfare Officers were appointed in areas where the needs of war workers were greatest. Eventually there were about 120 of these Welfare Officers.

In July, 1940, the Minister made the Factories (Medical and Welfare Services) Order which empowered the Chief Inspector of Factories to direct factories engaged on munitions production or on work on behalf of the Crown to make satisfactory arrangements for the medical and welfare supervision of their workpeople and for nursing and first-aid services. In 1944 there were 4,774 factories covered by the Order, each employing more than 250 persons, and special officers who might be called personnel managers or welfare supervisors were employed in 3,395. Perhaps the most striking development in factory welfare was the widespread increase in the provision of factory canteens. Before the war these numbered less than a thousand; by the end of the war, with government encouragement and persuasion fortified by directions made under various Orders, over 12,000 had been installed.

Hours of Work

In the early nineteenth century factory legislation was primarily concerned with regulating the hours, meal-times and holidays of children, young persons and women, and successive Factory Acts have continued to include provisions on these subjects. The statutory hours of work permitted for women and young persons under 18 have been steadily reduced and the 1937 Factories Act lays down a normal maximum working week of 48 hours as compared with the maxima laid down by the 1901 Act of 55½ hours in textile factories and 60 hours in non-textile factories. The Acts lay down limits in which the prescribed hours may be worked and go into considerable detail on such matters as rest breaks and exceptions to the normal maximum working week by overtime, for which maximum limits are laid down for the week, month and year. They also contain provisions permitting relatively unimportant variations in special circumstances.

The regulations for the employment of women and young persons in the Act could not be rigorously observed during the Second World War when the need for production demanded the fullest possible use of available manpower. The Minister was therefore given powers under Defence Regulations to issue Orders exempting factories from the requirements of the Act. Since the war, with the pressing need for production, particularly for export, and an acute shortage of labour, it has been found necessary to continue to authorise schemes of employment outside the limits of the Act. For example, many factories have found it advantageous to introduce part-time evening shifts which have proved to be popular with married women unable to undertake full-time employment and the Factories (Evening Employment) Order, 1950, has given power to inspectors to authorise such employment between 5 p.m. and 10 p.m.

Safety, Health and Welfare Standards

The great and continuous improvement in safety, health and welfare standards in industry in the last hundred years has not resulted solely from the provisions of factory legislation and the activities of the Factory Inspectorate. The way forward has been shown by progressive employers, and as their innovations have proved practicable it has been possible to carry legislation further, stage by stage. Perhaps the chief contribution of the Factory Inspectorate has been that, with its records of accidents and ill-health, its wide knowledge of conditions, and the insight into such matters acquired by it through experience, it has been able to guide the course of legislation in a practical and effective way.

Health hazards have been progressively eliminated or minimised. For example, the average number of cases of lead poisoning in all industries over the years 1952 to 1954 was 49 compared with 500 in 1910 to 1912. There has been outstanding progress in the prevention and elimination of dangerous dusts of all kinds; during the past 30 years the substitution of manufactured abrasive wheels for sandstone wheels in grinding processes and of non-siliceous materials for sand in blasting processes has greatly reduced the risk of silicosis. The practice among industrial firms of employing whole-time or part-time medical officers has grown. There were 35 such appointments on a whole-time basis and 70 on a part-time basis in 1939, and at the end of 1955 no fewer than 421 and 4,198 respectively. At the same time the number of factory nurses has increased.

Fifty years ago safeguards for machinery and plant or for working positions were added as an afterthought, and then often only under the threat of prosecution; today, to a great extent, they are planned beforehand. In many cases, makers, in consultation with the Factory Inspectorate, now incorporate machine safeguards additional to those required of them under the Acts in the design of new machinery. A significant contribution towards greater industrial safety is also made by many factories and by various voluntary bodies such as the Royal Society for the Prevention of Accidents. For the period of the Second World War, the Ministry entered into a special relationship with the industrial division of the Society, with the result that the activities of the latter were extended. Close co-operation between the Ministry and the Society continues. In many factories there are now committees composed of representatives of management and workers who discuss and advise on the problems of occupational health and of accident prevention; many firms also employ a safety officer to advise on safety matters. An indication of the improvement in safety arrangements in factories today is provided by the statistics relating to fatal accidents. During recent years the total number of fatalities in factories has averaged about 500 annually; 40 years ago, with many fewer people employed in industry, the average was about 950 annually.

The cumulative effect of the provisions of the Acts in preventing injury and ill-health and thus reducing loss of production is very considerable, but in addition to this they have tended to promote greater or better production in more positive ways. For example, the compulsory periodic examination of machinery and plant from the safety point of view has resulted in better general maintenance and fewer breakdowns. The fencing of machines and other safety precautions have sometimes led to the adoption of mechanical means of feeding machines or of conveying materials with consequent advantage to the rate of production. The introduction of mechanical exhaust ventilation has, in some instances, resulted in its becoming unnecessary to stop machines at frequent intervals to remove accumulations of dust, fluff and other particles. There is little doubt that the provisions for safety, health and welfare in factories must be regarded today as an important facet of the whole campaign for increased productivity.

Organisation

The Safety, Health and Welfare Department includes two administrative branches, and the Factory Inspectorate. One of the administrative branches deals primarily with industrial health and welfare problems, the other with safety, the regulation of hours of employment, and general questions arising under the Factories Acts.

The main function of the Administrative Department is to advise the Minister on the general policy by which safety, health and welfare standards in industry may be advanced, both through statutory and through voluntary means; and to carry out the general administration of the Factories Acts, and of Orders and Regulations made under these Acts. This function is discharged in close consultation with the Inspectorate. As a result of its comprehensive and regular inspection of those industrial establishments to which the Acts apply and its close contacts with industry, the Factory Inspectorate is able to advise the administration on the standards obtaining throughout industry and to draw attention to developments, such as the introduction of new processes or methods or materials of production, which may affect the safety and health of the worker and may call for legislation or for further exercise of the Minister's powers.

The Department maintains liaison with other Government Departments concerned with safety, health and welfare in employment not covered by the Factories Acts, such as coalmining, agriculture and shop and office employment, and with the Research Departments such as the Department of Scientific and Industrial Research and the Medical Research Council. It also deals with problems arising from the work of the International Labour Organisation and other international organisations on questions relating to safety, health and welfare.

The administrative branch dealing with industrial health matters was established in the Safety, Health and Welfare Department at the beginning of 1954. While the protection of the health of workers had for a very long time been one of the basic purposes of factory legislation, a greater emphasis was laid on health matters by various new provisions included in the 1937 and 1948 Factories Acts. These not only placed additional responsibilities on employers but also increased the powers and the duties of the Minister and the Department. At the same time, there was a growing awareness of the health hazards to which workers were exposed from harmful dusts and fumes, from the wide range of chemicals increasingly being used, and from radioactive substances. Although considerable progress was being made in combating these hazards through advances in both medical and technological knowledge, it was felt that more comprehensive measures of health protection were necessary in the light of the growing need. The Minister therefore decided in 1954, following discussions with industrial and medical organisations, to take steps to stimulate the further development of industrial health services in workplaces covered by the Factories Acts, including the provision of good environmental conditions at the place of work, of protection against industrial disease and poisoning, and of adequate medical and nursing supervision and first aid, and reappointed the Industrial Health Advisory Committee to advise him on this development. Its members are drawn from the two sides of industry, the Nationalised Industries, the medical and nursing professions, the Universities and local authorities. The general aim is to develop industrial health services on a voluntary basis, but the statutory powers in the Factories Acts are available for use as necessary. Surveys and field investigations are being promoted to determine where the industrial health services most need to be extended and also where further research is required. The administrative arrangements are the responsibility of the Safety, Health and Welfare Department working in conjunction with the Factory Inspectorate.

The branch of the Safety, Health and Welfare Department dealing with industrial safety has recently been closely associated with a general review of industrial accident prevention undertaken by the National Joint Advisory Council, which appointed a special Industrial Safety Sub-Committee for this purpose. The Report of the Sub-Committee, recommending ways and means of securing greater freedom from accidents at work, has been published. The numbers of accidents have shown little change in recent years and they cause an unnecessary drain on resources which the country can ill afford, apart from the pain and suffering they bring. It is hoped that the Report will contribute to a determined and effective attack on this problem throughout industry.

The Factory Inspectorate is now organised under the Chief Inspector assisted by five Deputy Chief Inspectors. The Inspectorate is some 400 strong and consists of a general Inspectorate, organised in 14 divisions and 97 districts throughout the country and three specialist branches—the medical branch, the engineering and chemical branch, and the electrical branch. A permanent exhibition of safety, health and welfare appliances of the latest and most efficient kind, set up in London in 1926 by the Home Office and now known as the Industrial Health and Safety Centre, is also staffed by the Inspectorate.

K

The bulk of inspection is carried out by the staff attached to the districts. Their duties are to see that the requirements of the Factories Acts and the various Regulations made under them are carried out. Some of the provisions of the Acts have been couched in general terms to enable the inspectors to press for progressively higher standards as practicable. The inspectors, in the course of their visits, may note many matters affecting the safety, health and welfare of the workers and report them with a view to further legislation or the widening of knowledge of such subjects. They always watch for innovations which may affect workers and they impress upon industry the need to take immediate precautions to meet any new risk: they may suggest a course of action immediately, or they may seek advice from the specialist branches or from other colleagues specially qualified to advise them.

An inspector has wide powers and has considerable freedom as to the manner in which he carries out his inspection visits. When making a visit, almost always unheralded, the inspector often calls at the factory office and meets the factory occupier or his manager who may accompany him on a tour of the works so that any points arising from the inspection can be discussed. If he has reason to believe that this practice would lessen the effectiveness of his visit, he may inspect parts of the works before announcing his arrival. He invariably talks with the workpeople and their representatives, asking women and young persons, for example, what hours they work and what breaks they get for refreshment and meals. Men and women may be asked about methods of cleaning, attending and approaching machinery in motion. The inspector also examines the various registers and documents which have to be maintained including, for example, the register of the medical examination of young persons and the reports of statutory examinations, such as those of boilers, lifts and cranes. If the visit is for the purpose of inquiring into an accident, the inspector discusses the circumstances of the accident with any worker who has witnessed it. At intervals inspectors make visits in the evenings, at night, and at week-ends, partly to check on the employment of women and young persons and partly to ensure that the provisions of the Acts are carried out during shift-working.

The Inspectorate takes pride in being a body whose work is to help the factory occupier to comply with the law and to run his factory on the lines of the best modern practice with respect to the safety, health and welfare of the employees. In 1943, the Minister, Mr Ernest Bevin, said at a Conference on Industrial Health: 'The Inspectors are well aware that the best results can be obtained from the willing co-operation of management and workpeople. . . . It is through persuasion, education and administration rather than threats that the work is done. But the sanctions remain there for the obdurate.'

New entrants to the Inspectorate have to satisfy the Civil Service Commissioners that they have suitable experience and educational qualifications. In general, candidates must be University graduates, preferably in engineering or science, although those with degrees in arts or other subjects are also eligible. If they have no University degree, candidates must have comparable technical qualifications in engineering or science, but the Commissioners may dispense with this requirement in the case of a candidate who appears to them to be exceptionally well fitted by reason of considerable works or other special practical experience. New inspectors are on probation for two years, at the end of which they are required to pass examinations in factory law and related matters. Difficulty has been experienced in recent years in recruiting as many inspectors with technical qualifications as was normal in the past, owing to the much greater demand for the services of such qualified people by industry and other employers.

The specialist medical, engineering and chemical and electrical branches study the medical and technical aspects of occupational health and safety problems and methods of dealing with them. In such studies the branches co-operate not only with each other and with the Inspectorate, but also with the appropriate professional bodies and with standing or *ad hoc* Committees representing employers and workers and, often, technical experts in individual industries. They also keep in touch with developments in other countries. Another function is to take part in the investigation of accidents and into the causes of ill-health involving technical problems of special difficulty; they assist the Inspectorate in carrying out its duties by giving advice, by taking some part in the inspection work and by visiting firms to discuss technical and medical problems. The medical branch, which is in the charge of the Senior Medical Inspector, undertakes field investigations into the causes and nature of occupational illnesses. It also exercises general supervision over the work of the Appointed Factory Doctors.

The staffing of the engineering and chemical branch has in the past been achieved by the promotion of suitably qualified inspectors from the general Inspectorate. Doctors and professionally qualified electrical engineers are recruited directly for the posts in the medical and electrical branches respectively. These two branches are organised on a decentralised basis. The engineering and chemical branch has in the past been stationed at the Ministry's Headquarters in London because of the greater degree of specialisation in its work.

The branch is largely concerned with new technical developments and it is essential that much of its work should be planned on a national basis and not be restricted geographically. It is planned in the future, however, to have engineering and chemical inspectors stationed also at Divisional Offices to relieve the Headquarters section of the branch of routine work.

Many aspects of the work of the specialist branches are reflected in the memoranda and pamphlets which the Ministry publishes on industrial safety, health and welfare. Many of the Committees referred to above have also made Reports which have been widely publicised. Some of the recommendations of the Committees have been given statutory effect; for example, those incorporated in the Codes of Regulations for Jute Factories and for Iron and Steel Foundries.

It is now usual to hold joint conferences on safety, health and welfare in industry with the representatives of employers and workers, or to set up advisory Committees for the purpose of such consultation and discussion. The Minister may discuss matters of general policy with the National Joint Advisory Council, or such discussions may be conducted by the administrative branches with the British Employers' Confederation and the Trades Union Congress or with national representatives of the employers and workers concerned. Representatives of the Inspectorate are usually present at such discussions, and on matters of a purely technical nature, discussions are arranged and conducted by the Inspectorate.

Industry, as always, is standing on the threshold of a new era. Whatever the industrial developments, e.g. in relation to atomic energy or automation, it will be the task of the Ministry to keep abreast of the new hazards which these developments bring in their train and, through the Factory Inspectorate, to ensure that management and workers alike take the measures needed to counter them.

PART IV

International Labour

CHAPTER XII

International Labour

*

THE international labour work of the Ministry covers all aspects of the work of the Department at home. All such work is centralised in the Overseas Department which normally represents the interests of all Departments of the Ministry in relations with international bodies. The work falls into four main categories; responsibility for the relations of Her Majesty's Government with the International Labour Organisation; representation of the Ministry's interests in regard to the activities of other international organisations; provision of Labour Attachés to United Kingdom Diplomatic Missions abroad; and the migration of labour to or from the United Kingdom.

The International Labour Organisation

A detailed account of the structure and activities of the International Labour Organisation would be out of place here, but a brief outline may be helpful as an introduction to an account of the work of the Ministry in maintaining relations with the Organisation.

The International Labour Organisation, now associated with the United Nations as one of the 'specialised agencies', was established under the Treaty of Versailles in 1919 and is one of the oldest international organisations operating today. The unique feature of the Organisation is its tripartite character—that is to say it provides for representation not only of governments but of employers and workers as well. Its declared aim is the promotion of social justice throughout the world by the establishment of humane conditions of labour. The present membership comprises 79 States.

The structure of the Organisation consists of the International Labour Conference, or General Conference, which is the sovereign body; the Governing Body, which is the executive council; and the International Labour Office, which is the permanent secretariat staffed by an international civil service under the control of the Director-General.

The main functions of the General Conference, which meets every year, are the formulation of international labour standards by the adoption of international instruments called Conventions or Recommendations, approval of the Organisation's annual budget, and the supervision of the implementation of Conventions by Member States. The Conference also acts as a world forum on labour matters and focuses attention, through its annual debates, on current problems of world-wide interest. Each Member State is entitled to be represented by four delegates, two of whom represent the Government and one each the employers and workers; these proportions of representation, which also apply in the Governing Body, give a balance of voting power which is a recognition of the fact that governments have the ultimate responsibility for accepting or rejecting Conventions or Recommendations adopted by the Conference and for giving effect to those which they accept, and that the funds of the Organisation are contributed by governments.

In addition to the General Conference, Regional Conferences are held from time to time, and a number of tripartite Industrial Committees meet to consider the problems of the main world industries. None of these has the power of adopting international instruments, which is entrusted to the General Conference. A number of standing Committees have also been established to advise the Organisation in its work in particular fields, such as labour statistics and juvenile employment, and *ad hoc* Committees of experts are frequently convened to advise on specific technical subjects.

The Governing Body plays an important part in formulating the policies and programmes of the Organisation. It fixes the agenda for the Conference and other meetings, controls the work of the International Labour Office and supervises the activities of the various specialised Committees. One of its most important functions is to make proposals to the Conference for the Organisation's annual budget. The Governing Body consists of 40 members. Of these, 20 are government representatives and 10 each are elected by the employers' and workers' delegates to the Conference. Ten of the government seats are held by representatives of the Member States of chief industrial importance, of which the United Kingdom is one.

The International Labour Office provides the secretariat and does the preparatory work for meetings of the Conference and the Governing Body and for all other I.L.O. meetings. It collects, analyses and distributes information on all matters coming within the scope of the Organisation. The Headquarters are in Geneva and there are, in addition, branch offices in London, Paris, Washington and other capitals, and national correspondents in many countries.

The work of the I.L.O. falls under three main headings—the formulation of international labour standards; the collection and dissemination of information; and operational activities, such as the provision of technical assistance and advice to governments desiring it. International labour standards take the form of Conventions or Recommendations adopted by the Conference, usually after discussion at two consecutive sessions. Since 1919 more than a hundred of each have been adopted on a wide variety of subjects, ranging from hours of work and minimum wage-fixing machinery to social policy in non-metropolitan territories. Over the years these have undoubtedly played an important part in raising labour standards throughout the world. The number of ratifications of Conventions by Member States is now over 1,800.

Information on a wide range of labour matters is obtained by the International Labour Office not only from the governments and employers' and workers' organisations in Member States but also through the branch offices and national correspondents throughout the world. It is then critically examined and made available either in reply to inquiries or in the various publications of the Office including the monthly *International Labour Review*.

The operational activities of the I.L.O. have grown rapidly in scope and importance since the end of the Second World War. In addition to its own programme the Organisation participates in the Expanded Technical Assistance Programme of the United Nations and assists Member States by advice on labour legislation or on other action to deal with such matters as employment service organisation, vocational and technical training, and industrial safety and health. This is done by a variety of means of which the principal are the sending out of advisory missions and the provision of fellowships for study or training abroad.

The Ministry's own connections with the I.L.O. date from the earliest days of the Organisation, when the Government decided that general responsibility for all United Kingdom business connected with it should be assigned to the Ministry. Two members of the Ministry played a large part in the formative work of setting up the Organisation and later joined its staff; they were the late Sir Harold Butler, appointed Deputy Director of the International Labour Office in 1920, and Director from 1932 to 1938, and Mr E. J. Phelan, who from 1941 to 1948 served first as Deputy Director and then as Director and afterwards Director-General. Throughout the Organisation's existence the Ministry, as representing the United Kingdom Government, has played a prominent part in its affairs. Sir Guildhaume Myrddin-Evans, one of the Ministry's Deputy Secretaries, has been the United Kingdom Government's representative on the Governing Body since 1945 and was its Chairman during the important post-war years from 1945 to 1947. Sir Guildhaume was again elected Chairman of the Governing Body and held this office in 1956–57. He was elected President of the 32nd Session of the General Conference held in 1949.

The Overseas Department deals with all I.L.O. matters and acts as the normal channel of communication between the International Labour Office and the United Kingdom Government. Much of the work involves frequent consultation, both with other interested branches in the Ministry and with other Government Departments which may have an interest in the particular subject. For example, the Government of the United Kingdom, in common with those of other Member States, might be asked for its views on a draft Recommendation on welfare facilities which had been prepared by the International Labour Office for discussion at the next Session of the Conference. The Ministry's own Safety, Health and Welfare Department would have the main interest in this subject, but there would be many others to be consulted, especially if the scope of the proposed instrument were fairly wide. Thus the Home Departments might have views to express about it in relation to shops and other non-industrial employment, the Agricultural Departments in regard to agriculture, the Ministry of Power in regard to mines and quarries, and so on. The subject would also have to be considered in its possible application to British territories overseas and for this purpose the Colonial Office would be the Department mainly concerned; and since the final view is to be that of the United Kingdom Government, and not that of Great Britain alone, the Ministry of Labour and National Insurance in Northern Ireland would be consulted. It is also usual to afford the British Employers' Confederation and the Trades Union Congress, as the representative organisations of employers and workers respectively, the opportunity of making comments.

Consultations like this are generally necessary for each of the technical items on the agenda of the Conference, both when governments are asked for comments on the reports prepared for the Conference by the International Labour Office and subsequently when briefs are being prepared for the guidance of the Government Delegation attending the Conference. A similar procedure is followed as regards subjects coming up for consideration at sessions of the Governing Body or other meetings at which the United Kingdom Government is to be represented.

Another side of the work is concerned with the Conventions and Recommendations adopted by the International Labour Conference. These are not automatically binding upon Member States, but each Government is required, under the I.L.O. Constitution, to bring them promptly to the notice of the competent authority—in this country Parliament—for any appropriate action. This means that proposals upon each instrument adopted are formulated in consultation with the other branches and Departments concerned and, after approval by the Government, are published in the form of a White Paper and presented to Parliament. In the case of Conventions, the White Paper may indicate the Government's intention either to ratify on the basis of existing legislation or practice, or to introduce legislation so as to make ratification possible or, for reasons stated, to take no further action. In the case of Recommendations no question of ratification arises, but the usual practice is to give a reasoned statement of the extent to which the Government regards the particular Recommendation as acceptable.

If the Government ratifies a Convention, it is required under the I.L.O. Constitution to submit an annual report on its application and enforcement. These reports are prepared by the Department directly responsible for the particular subject, but the Overseas Department of the Ministry has a general responsibility for the reports and for seeing that they adequately discharge the Government's obligations under the I.L.O. Constitution. At the present time the number of Conventions ratified by the United Kingdom Government is 54; in addition to the annual reports covering the United Kingdom, over 1,800 reports are submitted each year (through the Colonial Office, the Commonwealth Relations Office and the Home Office) by the governments of non-metropolitan territories to which the Conventions are applied. With the reports also required on unratified Conventions and on Recommendations (governments have to report each year on a group of these specially selected for the purpose by the Governing Body), the total number of reports to be collected, scrutinised and forwarded annually is now about 1,900 and this number will continue to grow as more Conventions are ratified by the United Kingdom Government and applied to the non-metropolitan territories.

There is also the practical business of arranging for United Kingdom representation at I.L.O. meetings of all kinds. Apart from the Conference itself, in a normal year there are three meetings of the Governing Body, three of Industrial Committees and some half a dozen other meetings at which the United Kingdom is represented. Many of the meetings take place at Geneva, but meetings may be held elsewhere in Europe or in Asia or America. Where government representatives have to be sent from the United Kingdom the responsibility for seeing that the necessary arrangements for travel, finance and accommodation are made rests upon the Overseas Department.

Members of the Department may themselves be called upon to serve as government delegates or advisers in the United Kingdom delegation to the Conference, to accompany the United Kingdom Government Member to meetings of the Governing Body, or to act as government delegates at meetings of Industrial Committees or other bodies. In this capacity their work has much in common with that of government representatives at other international meetings. The same techniques are needed for preparing the ground, for negotiation with and enlisting the support of other delegations, for expounding the United Kingdom Government's point of view in debate and, on occasion, for judicious compromise or change of tactics in order to secure the best possible result. But there is one important difference. The tripartite character of the I.L.O. means that the views of the employers' and workers' groups, as well as those of other governments, have to be taken into account. The employers' and workers' delegates in a national delegation are free to vote individually and may, and often do, vote differently from the delegates of their government or from one another. The various employers' and workers' delegates from the countries represented form themselves into separate groups, each of which may agree beforehand the way in which the votes of members of the group shall be cast. Informal contact is maintained with the employers' and workers' groups, and especially with the representatives of the United Kingdom employers and workers who are influential within their own groups. Such contacts can do a great deal to ease the course of the discussions and help in securing a generally acceptable solution.

The most important event in the I.L.O. calendar is, of course, the annual session of the Conference, which normally takes place in Geneva during June and lasts about three weeks. The United Kingdom delegation consists of two government delegates and one each of employers and workers, each delegate being accompanied by a number of advisers. The delegates and advisers are appointed by the Minister. The employers' and workers' elements in the delegation are nominated, in accordance with the I.L.O. Constitution, in agreement with the most representative organisations—the British Employers' Confederation and the Trades Union Congress respectively. The advisers to the government delegates come from the Overseas Department and from the Departments concerned with the different 'technical' items on the agenda; in general, each has his own part to play, under the directions of the government delegates, in the detailed discussions of particular items in Committee. The practical arrangements for the whole delegation—including any necessary arrangements for travel, finance and accommodation—are undertaken by the Overseas Department and are carried out by a secretary (or joint secretaries) to the delegation appointed for the purpose.

It is a well established tradition that the Minister, like the Ministers of Labour from many other countries, attends for a part of the Conference and contributes to the debate on the Director-General's Report. This normally deals with the world labour situation in general, or with some particular topic of current interest. The Minister subsequently presents to Parliament, in the form of a White Paper, a report by the government delegates on the Conference, which contains a brief account of the proceedings and the texts of any Conventions, Recommendations and Resolutions adopted.

The I.L.O.'s operational activities, particularly the technical assistance it provides, have already been mentioned. In addition to its financial contribution the United Kingdom collaborates by accepting I.L.O. Fellows for study or training either within the Ministry or outside, in many cases in industry, and by finding experts, from the Civil Service or elsewhere, to undertake advisory missions in the under-developed countries. All arrangements in regard to Fellows and experts, except for minor material arrangements, are made through the Overseas Department.

It is convenient to mention here, although this is distinct from the technical assistance provided by the International Labour Organisation, the Technical Co-operation Scheme of the Colombo Plan for the economic development of countries in South and South-East Asia under which technical assistance is given to countries in that area. The Ministry co-operates with the Commonwealth Relations Office in recruiting experts for assignment to countries needing help and by arranging with employers in this country for industrial training to be given to trainees nominated by the Asian governments.

The Ministry's relationship with other International Organisations

A number of the international organisations set up since the 1939–45 war deal with problems that are of interest to the Ministry either because of its domestic responsibilities or because of its responsibility for United Kingdom relations with the I.L.O. Among the world organisations, the United Nations, and in particular its Economic and Social Council, is concerned with a great variety of economic and social subjects; for example, with the economic and social rights of the individual, with industrial productivity, and with technical assistance for economic development. Various Specialised Agencies associated with the United Nations, such as the United Nations Educational, Scientific and Cultural Organisation, the World Health Organisation, and the Food and Agriculture Organisation, deal with specific questions touching on such matters as vocational guidance or training, or industrial hygiene, which have an interest both for the Ministry and for the I.L.O.

Of the regional organisations, the Organisation for European Economic Co-operation has established a Manpower Committee which is concerned with means to ensure the fullest and most effective use of manpower and deals with such problems as the freer movement of workers across national boundaries, employment service organisation, vocational training and the dilution of skilled labour. The Council of Europe has a more general mandate, its purpose being 'to achieve greater unity between its members for the purpose of . . . facilitating their economic and social progress . . . by discussion of questions of common concern and by agreements and common action in economic, social . . . and administrative matters and in the maintenance and further realisation of human rights'. Within narrower geographical limits, the Western European Union, which in 1955 superseded the Brussels Treaty Organisation, seeks to 'develop on corresponding lines the social and other related services' of the Member countries and to raise the standards of living of their peoples. The North Atlantic Treaty Organisation, too, in addition to its purely defensive object, has a general interest in economic progress, and concerns itself with problems of labour movement as well as the elimination of manpower shortages hindering defence production.

The general responsibility for the relations of Her Majesty's Government with these organisations rests with the Foreign Office or, in the case of the Specialised Agencies, with such Departments as the Ministry of Education and the Ministry of Health for U.N.E.S.C.O. and the World Health Organisation respectively. The Overseas Department represents the views of the Ministry to these Departments on matters arising in the international organisations which touch on the Ministry's field of interest, and provides information asked for by the organisations about industrial and social practices in this country. In addition to co-operating in this way in the briefing of delegations to meetings of the organisations, the Ministry, in certain cases, provides the personnel of the delegation. Officers of the Ministry regularly represent the United Kingdom on the Manpower Committee of O.E.E.C., Working Groups set up for labour questions by the North Atlantic Treaty Organisation, the Social Committee established to advise the Committee of Ministers of the Council of Europe, the Western European Union Social Committee and certain of its Sub-Committees and its Joint Committee on the Rehabilitation and Resettlement of the Disabled; from time to time delegates are provided for other Committees. The opportunity thus afforded for the exchange of experience and the consideration of common problems with senior officials of corresponding Departments abroad is one of the most valuable features of discussions in these inter-governmental organisations.

Labour Attachés

The Labour Attaché is a comparatively recent addition to the staffs of Diplomatic Missions as explained in Chapters I and II.

Labour Attachés are responsible to, and work under the direction of, the Head of the Mission and advise him on subjects within their competence. Another part of their duty is to ensure that important developments in the labour and industrial fields are fully and currently reported. Their reports may be included in a dispatch from the Head of the Mission to the Foreign Office or Commonwealth Relations Office, or may be sent direct to the Ministry where technical questions are concerned. They are also called upon from time to time to give information on conditions in the United Kingdom, or upon British policy and practice on a wide range of labour and social questions to official, trade union, or employers' representatives in the countries to which they are assigned. In addition, they assist in making arrangements for foreign or Commonwealth visitors who wish to come to the United Kingdom to study British practice in the labour, social or industrial field, and for British visitors and delegations who make corresponding visits to the countries in which they are stationed.

Wide knowledge and experience of industrial relations and social administration are a desirable, if not an essential, qualification for Labour Attachés if they are to establish useful contacts with representative organisations and persons in the field of labour and social affairs and to gain their confidence. For this reason Labour Attachés are normally senior officers of the Ministry, which bears the cost of their appointments. The appointments are made in co-operation with the Foreign Office or Commonwealth Relations Office, and are for a period which is not less than two years and is frequently longer; the Labour Attaché may then return to Departmental duties at home and be replaced by another officer of the Ministry. There are now 18 Labour Attachés in post at Missions in North, Central and South America, Europe, the Middle East and Asia. In some cases they have responsibility for neighbouring countries as well as the country in which they are stationed. In all, 52 countries are covered.

Reports from Labour Attachés enable the Ministry to have up-to-date details on labour and social legislation and administrative practices in other countries and to compare these with British developments. They also give information on various labour and social matters which may be under consideration in international bodies such as the International Labour Organisation.

At intervals of about two years the Labour Attachés are called together for conference at the Ministry. Such conferences provide a valuable opportunity for the exchange of information on overseas labour matters and for extending and refreshing the knowledge of Labour Attachés, on developments at home about which they should be fully informed.

Migration of Labour to or from the United Kingdom

The functions of the Overseas Department under this heading relate to the admission of persons from overseas for employment in this country, or the departure of persons in this country for employment or settlement overseas.

This Department is responsible for dealing with applications from foreigners for permission to take employment in this country. Under the provisions of the Aliens Order, 1953—the latest embodiment of regulations which have been operative for nearly 40 years—a foreigner may not be permitted to enter the country for employment unless he has a permit granted by the Minister to his employer. Permission must also be obtained before a foreigner who originally entered the country as a student or visitor may take up employment. A large number of permits are issued for employment in domestic work, and applications for permission are also received for the employment of foreigners in a wide variety of industries and occupations. Special arrangements are made to facilitate the employment of student-trainees from abroad who desire to come to this country for a limited period to improve their knowledge and experience. Other special arrangements apply to particular groups such as foreign artistes and entertainers who come here to undertake specific engagements. In view of the variety of applications the criteria for the grant of permits must vary in detail, but the general conditions are that the proposed employment is reasonable and necessary and that adequate efforts have been made by the employer to find suitable workers among British subjects or foreigners long resident in the country. The wages and other conditions proposed must be not less favourable than those commonly accorded to British workers. Subject to these conditions, consideration is given to individual cases according to their particular circumstances. These arrangements apply in cases where an employer has made his own contact with a foreign worker and asks for him individually. The Department also places facilities at the disposal of employers who desire to recruit foreign workers in appreciable numbers from countries abroad, especially Italy, to fill vacancies in undermanned industries and services.

Many people who leave the country for employment or settlement abroad do so under private arrangements. The Ministry is, however, called upon from time to time to assist Commonwealth Governments who desire to increase the numbers of immigrants from this country generally or in particular occupations. While the manpower needs of industry must be taken into account, it is the Government's declared policy to encourage migration to Commonwealth countries and the Department therefore gives whatever help may be needed by Commonwealth authorities in London in arranging for publicity, recruiting boards and selection interviews. In particular, it helps to determine the eligibility of applicants for assistance under the Australian Assisted Passage Scheme, to which the British Government makes a financial contribution. In addition, the Overseas Department administers a service centrally for employers who wish to engage personnel for overseas vacancies.

PART V

Statistics

CHAPTER XIII

Statistics

*

WHEN the Ministry was set up at the end of 1916 it was charged with the duty, formerly carried out by the Board of Trade, of collecting and publishing labour statistics. The statistics collected were intended to provide reliable and impartial information for the public, particularly workpeople, employers, trade unions and students. As labour legislation widened in scope, the information collected served also as a basis on which to found the Government's economic and social policies in matters concerning labour.

The Ministry now collects and publishes a wide range of labour statistics. These deal mainly with the general manpower position, employment and unemployment, rates of wages, hours and earnings, industrial disputes, industrial accidents and diseases, and retail prices. The statistics are published in the *Ministry of Labour Gazette*[1] which has been issued in unbroken sequence since 1893. Some of the principal statistics compiled by the Ministry are also included in the *Monthly Digest of Statistics*, the *Annual Abstract of Statistics*, and *Economic Trends* issued by the Central Statistical Office, and in certain publications of the International Labour Office and of the United Nations.

Most of the subjects on which statistics and information are collected by the Statistics Department of the Ministry fall into the following groups:—employment and unemployment, wage-rates, hours and earnings; the index of retail prices; industrial disputes; trade union membership; and labour matters overseas. The responsibility for information needed primarily for employment policy purposes rests with the Employment Policy Department of the Ministry.

Employment and Unemployment
At regular intervals information is published in the *Gazette* about the numbers in employment classified according to industry and

[1] After changing its title in 1905 to the *Board of Trade Labour Gazette* it became again the *Labour Gazette* in 1917 and finally from 1922 the *Ministry of Labour Gazette*.

sex; the extent of short-time and overtime working in the manufacturing industries; the numbers unemployed analysed according to industry, region (with details regarding certain large towns), sex and duration of unemployment; labour turnover; and the numbers of placings in employment and of notified vacancies remaining unfilled.

The figures of the numbers in employment and unemployed and of the numbers of employers and workers on their own account, together with the numbers in the Armed Forces and Women's Forces, are added together to provide estimates of the total working population. The broad industrial analysis of the figures thus obtained is also published in the *Gazette*.

The practice of compiling statistics of the total working population was started early in the 1939–45 war to assist in manpower planning. Detailed 'Manpower Surveys' were made at regular intervals; estimates were made of the manpower requirements of the Forces and of the munitions and other industries, and complementary estimates were made at the same time of the numbers of men and women who could be taken from the less essential industries or from the non-employed population to meet these requirements. Manpower 'Budgets' were drawn up showing on the one hand the various demands for labour and on the other hand the various sources of supply. On the basis of these budgets a system of 'allocation' was evolved for the purpose of regulating the withdrawal of men and women from the various sources of supply and allocating them systematically to the Forces and the vital industries.

The Ministry bases its employment statistics partly on returns obtained from employers and partly on information gained from a count of contribution cards of persons covered by the National Insurance Scheme. The practice of collecting information from employers about the numbers of workers employed was extended in 1940 when it was found that information obtained from the exchange of contribution cards was neither frequent enough nor comprehensive enough to provide the estimates of the working population necessary for the manpower surveys. Powers were therefore given to the Ministry under Defence Regulations to obtain information from employers. At the end of the war it was decided to continue the arrangement for obtaining returns from employers in order to obtain statistics on which the Government could base its full employment policy, and permanent powers for that purpose were obtained under the Statistics of Trade Act, 1947. The returns, rendered on what are known as 'L' forms, are obtained monthly from all employers in manufacturing industries with 100 or more employees and a quarter of the employers in those industries with 11–99 employees and from a sample of employers in the distributive and catering trades and certain other services. Information about industries not covered by these returns is obtained from other sources, such as the Ministry of Power for coalmining and the Ministry of Works for building and contracting.

Until July, 1948, the exchange of cards bearing unemployment contributions was undertaken by the Ministry and although there had been many changes in the scope of the Unemployment Insurance Scheme since the statistical series based on it began in 1923, it had been possible to maintain a reasonable comparability in the figures over the years. This had been achieved partly by obtaining estimates from other sources of groups not covered by the insurance scheme and partly by the separate classification of new groups coming into insurance. In July, 1948, the series of manpower statistics was radically affected by two unrelated but coinciding changes. The first was the introduction of the new National Insurance Scheme which extended unemployment insurance to all paid employees and to employers and to the self-employed (large classes of employees had been excluded from the scope of the old unemployment insurance scheme). The second was that the industrial coding system used in the Ministry was replaced by a Standard Industrial Classification, designed by an Inter-departmental Government Committee for use by all Government Departments. Together these changes[1] laid the foundation for a wider basis of manpower statistics and a more detailed industrial analysis, but the immediate effect was to destroy comparability with the old series of statistics.

It was desirable, apart from the change in industrial coding, that the Ministry should issue statistics in the same form as previously. To achieve this a number of administrative problems had to be solved in co-operation with the Ministry of National Insurance. For example, the new insurance scheme was designed to cover all insurable contingencies by means of combined contributions, with the result that unemployed insurance cards were superseded by comprehensive cards issued and exchanged by the Ministry of National Insurance. Moreover changes had to be made in the method of exchanging contribution cards. Under the old unemployment insurance scheme all cards were exchanged simultaneously at the middle of each year, but owing to the large increase in the number of cards under the new scheme it was decided to exchange

[1] See *Ministry of Labour Gazette* for February and April, 1949, and February, 1951, for more details of these changes. To provide the only comparison possible between the old and the new scheme the *Gazette* for April, 1949, contains an analysis on the basis of the old industrial classification of the numbers at mid-1948 who were previously insured under the Unemployment Insurance Acts.

them in four quarterly (and equal) parts in March, June, September and December. Mid-year estimates of the employed population continue to be made on the basis of detailed analyses of the numbers of cards exchanged in June, supplemented by returns from employers with five or more employees showing the total numbers of cards held by them in respect of their employees.

For employers and workers on their own account the figures of cards exchanged are to some extent incomplete, but these are supplemented by information from other sources, notably the Census of Population.

As regards unemployment, the principal source of information is a monthly return, obtained from each of the Ministry's local offices, giving an industrial analysis of the numbers of persons registered as unemployed on a particular day in the month. Supplementary analyses according to age, occupation and duration of unemployment are obtained at less frequent intervals. Each month returns are also obtained from the local offices to show, for each industry, the number of employment vacancies that have been filled, and the numbers that have been notified but have not yet been filled.

Wage-Rates, Hours and Earnings

In the great majority of industries in the United Kingdom minimum, or standard, time-rates of wages for wage-earners have been fixed by voluntary collective agreements between organisations of employers and workpeople or by statutory orders. Particulars of these rates and the standard working hours, and of the changes occurring, are collected regularly by the Ministry and published monthly in the *Gazette*. This information is supplemented twice a year by the publication of statistics of the average actual earnings and hours of work of manual wage-earners in a large number of industries. The local offices of the Ministry have no part in the collection of wages statistics, the information being obtained directly by the Statistics Department at Headquarters.

Wages statistics date back to the early days of the Labour Department of the Board of Trade and the *Gazette*; and some of the series began even earlier. Since those days the growth of wage-negotiating machinery, both voluntary and statutory, has resulted in many more classes of workers being included in the statistics; and the greater standardisation of wages, through the tendency towards national rather than local bargaining, has also meant that the published information covers many more workers.

Over the years the Statistics Department has developed useful arrangements, with both the voluntary and statutory wage negotiating bodies, for the notification of new agreements or changes in

existing agreements. This information is used to compile the tables
of current rates published annually in the volume *Time Rates of
Wages and Hours of Labour*; changes between volumes are notified
monthly in the *Gazette*. The first volume in this series was issued in
1893 and a further eight appeared at irregular intervals between then
and 1946; since then publication has been made yearly except for
1953. Since 1950, details of rates of pay for young persons, of overtime rates, and of holidays with pay have been set out in three
separate appendices. The volumes record the minimum or standard
time-rates (including basic piece-rates where known) and hours but
contain no derived statistics; the information published in the
Gazette shows the principal changes in rates of wages and hours
from which the annual volume can be kept up to date, and also
analyses the effect of all reported changes and estimates the total
number of workpeople affected and the total net amount of the
change on their weekly rates of wages. From time to time articles
have been published in the *Gazette* summarising information
contained in the various agreements and statutory orders on such
subjects as payment of wages for holidays, local variation in wage-
rates, and hours of labour and overtime rates.

The index of Rates of Wages, which is regularly published in the
Gazette, measures the movement, from month to month, in the
level of full-time weekly rates of wages in the principal industries
and services in the United Kingdom. The index is based on the
recognised rates of wages fixed by collective agreements, arbitration
awards or statutory orders; it does not reflect changes in earnings
due to alterations in working hours, variations in piece-work earnings
or other causes. The method of calculation makes allowance for the
relative numerical strength of the industries; from time to time a new
series is started to take account of significant changes and also to
extend the coverage. The first series dates from 1880 and the eighth
series dates from January, 1956. Although the individual series are
not absolutely comparable, those from 1920, if linked together,
give a broad indication of the movement in weekly wage-rates over
the period.

The statistics of wage-rates, useful though they are for many
purposes, do not give a picture of actual earnings. They take no
account, for instance, of overtime or short-time working or bonuses.
The Ministry obtains information about earnings by postal inquiry
from a large sample of employers in the United Kingdom in April
and October each year. The results are published in the *Gazette*,
usually in the following September and March, in the form of an
analysis of average weekly and hourly earnings and average hours
worked by manual wage-earners in the manufacturing industries

and some other industry groups. The first earnings inquiry was in 1886 and there was a second in 1906. The results of these inquiries which analysed the average earnings by occupation, were published in separate volumes but summarised in the *Abstract of Labour Statistics*. Other inquiries followed at lengthy intervals but it was not until 1942 that these arrangements for earnings returns on a voluntary basis were put on a regular half-yearly footing. The employers are asked for statements of total wages and total hours worked separately for men, women, boys and girls; no attempt has been made except in 1938 to obtain details of the wages paid to individual workers and no details of earnings in particular occupations have been collected since 1906. In certain of the more recent inquiries, however, additional information has been collected regarding the numbers of workers remunerated by time-rates and the numbers remunerated by piece-work arrangements, output bonus schemes and other arrangements under which pay varies according to individual or collective output. Some information has also been collected about the numbers and proportions of those working under various shift-work systems. The returns received cover about 7 million wage-earners or rather more than two-thirds of the total wage-earners in the industries included in the inquiry. As the proportion covered differs in different industries the figures for each industry have since 1938 been weighted by the approximate number of workers employed by all the firms in the industry to provide the average earnings and hours of work for groups of industries and also the average for all industries combined.

The comparability with earlier dates of the earnings figures, industry by industry, was impaired by the introduction of the Standard Industrial Classification in 1948; the combined average is not, of course, affected.

An index figure for earnings is also published with the results of each inquiry for comparison with the wage-rates index; this figure is used extensively in wage claims.

At the present time the only official statistics of salaries are estimates made by the Central Statistical Office from various sources and published annually in the White Paper on National Income and Expenditure. The Ministry has recently started the collection of some information from which it is hoped it may be possible to produce general indices of changes in salary rates and in the average earnings of salaried employees in a number of industries and services taken together.

Up to the outbreak of war in 1939 statistics were collected at annual intervals from all undertakings known to be operating employee profit-sharing or co-partnership schemes. An analysis of the progress of such schemes and of their financial benefits to employees was published annually in the *Gazette*. Because of renewed interest in the post-war period, statistics of schemes in operation in 1954 were collected in 1955 and the results were published in the May, 1956, issue of the *Gazette*.

Index of Retail Prices: Industrial Disputes: Trade Union Membership: Labour Matters Overseas

Official cost-of-living index figures were introduced during the 1914–18 war to determine the percentage increase month by month in the cost of maintaining unchanged the standard of living prevailing among working-class households in 1914. These index figures, published monthly in the *Gazette*, became of great importance in industrial relations, because of the growth of the practice of relating wage changes, or claims for wage changes, to changes in the index.

During 1937 and 1938, the Ministry carried out an inquiry to obtain information about the current distribution of working-class expenditure, mainly for the purpose of revising the cost-of-living index.[1] The inquiry covered more than 10,000 households of manual workers in general and non-manual workers with wages or salaries not exceeding £250 a year. By the time the results were available, war had broken out and all plans for revising the index had to be postponed. During the war there was a further substantial change in spending habits and the index, based on 1914 standards, became seriously unrepresentative of wage-earners' expenditure. In August, 1946, the Minister appointed a Cost of Living Advisory Committee. Its first Report, issued in March, 1947, recommended that the old index should be discontinued and that until new budgets could be collected to provide the basis for a more permanent index, a new interim index should be prepared, based on the wider pattern of expenditure shown by the 1937–38 budget inquiry. The task of preparing the interim index was entrusted to a Technical Committee, and the new interim index was brought into use as from June, 1947, with prices at that date taken as 100. In December, 1950, the Advisory Committee was called together again and its second and third Reports were issued in August, 1951, and March, 1952. Following the acceptance of the recommendations of these Reports, arrangements were made for a comprehensive household expenditure inquiry covering a sample of the whole community and spread over a full year, to provide a basis for a new index. Meanwhile a number of modifications were introduced in the interim index to relate it

[1] A description of the methods and results of the inquiry can be found in the *Ministry of Labour Gazette* for December, 1940, January, 1941, and February, 1941.

more closely to the post-war spending habits of the average working-class household.

The new inquiry began in January, 1953. During the following twelve months nearly 20,000 addresses representative of all types of household in the United Kingdom were visited and about 13,000 complete households co-operated by supplying details of their spending. A comprehensive Report on the inquiry was published in October, 1957. Before the publication of the Report some of the more important statistics resulting from the inquiry were studied by the Cost of Living Advisory Committee which submitted a Report to the Minister in March 1956. In this Report it was recommended that the interim index should be terminated immediately and that a new index of retail prices should be started, to measure changes in the average level of prices compared with the level at January, 1956, taken as 100. This index would be based on the average expenditure pattern revealed by the 1953 expenditure inquiry, except that it would exclude information supplied by certain high-income households and by households mainly or wholly dependent on National Insurance retirement pensions and/or National Assistance paid in supplementation or instead of such pensions. The Report contained detailed plans for the new index, and the Government accepted the recommendations in the Report. The new index is now in operation.[1] Information as to the prices of the large number of commodities and services needed for calculating the index each month is collected mainly by personal visits by local officers of the Ministry or by postal inquiries from the Ministry's Headquarters.

In some industries agreements provide that basic wage-rates shall move up or down automatically with changes in the Index of Retail Prices. Such agreements do not preclude the trade unions concerned from negotiating changes in wages or conditions on other grounds. Existing sliding scale arrangements cover about 2 million workers. In 1957, they were responsible for 7·2 per cent of the total net weekly increase in rates of wages.

A monthly review of industrial disputes involving stoppages of work is published in the *Gazette*, such disputes being defined as those connected with terms of employment or conditions of labour. The information is collected from the parties to the dispute and other sources, and no attempt is made to distinguish between 'official' and 'unofficial' stoppages, or between strikes and lockouts, owing to the difficulty of defining these terms in such a way that the information available would permit of separate classification.

[1] A full account of the basis and calculation of the retail prices index is given in the publication *Method of Construction and Calculation of the Index of Retail Prices*, published by H.M.S.O., price 1s. 9d. net.

The published figures show the number of stoppages, the number of workers affected, and the aggregate number of working days lost by those workers. The figures are also analysed to show the principal causes of the stoppages and their duration; stoppages lasting less than a day, or involving less than 10 workpeople, are excluded, except when they involve a total loss of over 100 working days. More comprehensive statistics are published in an annual review, usually in the May issue of the *Gazette*.

Statistics of the total membership of trade unions are published annually in the *Gazette*. The figures include not only the unions registered with the Registrars of Friendly Societies under the Trade Union Acts, but also unregistered unions. The figures are analysed according to the industry group in which the majority of each union's members are employed and according to the size of the unions, and are shown separately for men and women.

The Ministry also publishes a Directory of Employers' Associations, Trade Unions, Joint Organisations, etc., which is periodically revised.

From its earliest days the *Gazette* has also published statistics relating to labour matters overseas obtained from the study of overseas publications. The setting up of the International Labour Office in 1920 provided a central source for much of the material previously studied at first hand and at the same time increased the demand for information about labour matters in this country for overseas consumption. The international exchange of information has greatly expanded with the formation of new international bodies concerned with social and economic affairs since the war and the attachment of officers of the Ministry as Labour Attachés to British Missions overseas.

The Organisation of Statistical Work in the Ministry

Statistical work in the Ministry is undertaken chiefly in the Statistics Department. The work of the three divisions of the Statistics Department does not differ in essentials from that of any other Departments of Statistics, however much it may differ in subject-matter. There are decisions to be taken regarding the feasibility of presenting information on a given subject, the choice of method of collection of data, arrangements for collection and compilation and the interpretation of results. Much of the work of compilation and analysing is mechanised. In 1935, punched-card machinery for the mechanical sorting and tabulation of statistics was introduced and this made possible a more varied analysis and comparison of statistical material. Where it is advantageous, keyboard calculating machines are used for arithmetical calculation.

There is a Standing Committee in the Ministry responsible for statistics. All existing and projected statistical returns are examined by this Committee to make sure that the various administrative branches are not asking for returns unnecessarily or in greater detail than is essential and that no statistical return is continued if it has served its purpose. The *Ministry of Labour Gazette* is edited in the Statistics Department and all three divisions contribute to it. Contributions are also obtained from other Departments of the Ministry. Each issue of the *Gazette* has a leading article on some particular aspect of labour with which the Ministry is concerned and other articles of topical interest; for example, on recent labour legislation, or reports of Conferences and Committees. In addition, summaries are given of arbitration awards, statutory notices and orders, and official publications.

PART VI

The Organisation of the Department

CHAPTER XIV

Organisation and Structure of the Ministry

*

THE division of responsibility within the Ministry follows the customary pattern for major Departments of State in this country. The Minister, who is a member of the Cabinet and the political head of the Ministry, is responsible to Parliament for the Ministry's policy and conduct; he is assisted by a Parliamentary Secretary. The Permanent Secretary, as head of the staff of civil servants, is responsible for the Ministry's organisation and efficiency and for advising the Minister on matters of policy; the decisions on all major policy issues are taken by the Minister. On most matters the evolution of policy is a complex process to which many influences contribute —the general views of the Government of the day; the Minister's own plans; the views of officials, both in the Ministry and in other Government Departments likely to be affected, on what is practicable or wise; and the opinions of the Advisory Councils and Committees which have grown to be an essential part of the consultative organisation of the Ministry.

Headquarters Organisation

The Minister has a Private Office and he and the Parliamentary Secretary each has a private secretary, of principal officer and assistant principal rank respectively. The private secretaries are responsible for the control of the executive and clerical staff in the Private Office, and are concerned with all matters appropriate to the Minister and the Parliamentary Secretary by virtue of their position as members of the Government as distinct from as Members of Parliament. Politically, the Minister and the Parliamentary Secretary are each assisted by a Parliamentary Private Secretary who is a Member of Parliament.

The work at Headquarters is divided between 12 Departments (see chart on page 178). The Industrial Relations Department is in the charge of the Chief Industrial Commissioner, whose post is on a level with that of a Deputy Secretary and who also has oversight over the Statistics Department. The remaining policy Departments, as well as the Organisation and Establishments Department and the

M

ORGANISATION OF THE MINISTRY OF LABOUR AND NATIONAL SERVICE AT 1ST JANUARY, 1958

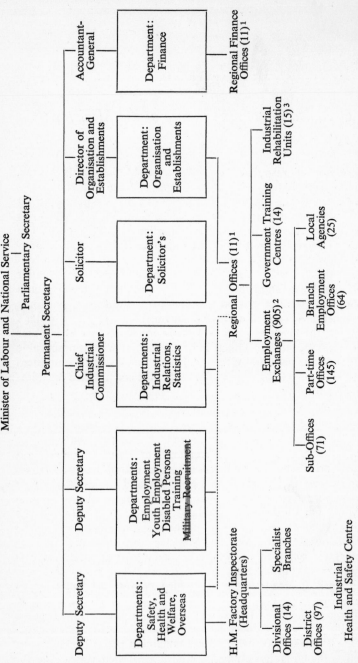

Minister of Labour and National Service

Parliamentary Secretary

Parliamentary Secretary

Permanent Secretary

Deputy Secretary — Chief Industrial Commissioner — Solicitor — Director of Organisation and Establishments — Accountant-General

Deputy Secretary

Deputy Secretary

Departments: Safety, Health and Welfare, Overseas

Departments: Employment, Youth Employment, Disabled Persons, Training, Military Recruitment

Departments: Industrial Relations, Statistics

Department: Solicitor's

Department: Organisation and Establishments

Department: Finance

H.M. Factory Inspectorate (Headquarters)

Divisional Offices (14)

District Offices (97)

Specialist Branches

Industrial Health and Safety Centre

Regional Offices (11) [1]

Sub-Offices (71)

Part-time Offices (145)

Employment Exchanges (905) [2]

Branch Employment Offices (64)

Local Agencies (25)

Government Training Centres (14)

Industrial Rehabilitation Units (15) [3]

Regional Finance Offices (11) [1]

[1] Includes Scotland and Wales. Each of the 11 Regional Offices includes a Regional Nursing Appointments Office.
[2] One hundred and sixty-five exchanges include Nursing Appointments Offices affording facilities for placing those seeking posts as nurses or midwives; 48 exchanges provide specialised service for those seeking professional or executive posts; 19 exchanges deal with deferment of National Service for agricultural workers.

Finance Department, are in the charge of Under-Secretaries. In general the Departments are divided into branches and each branch into divisions. The head of a branch is normally of assistant secretary or equivalent rank and the head of a division of principal officer or equivalent rank. The organisation of the Solicitor's Department is described in Chapter XV and that of the Factory Inspectorate, which is a part of the Safety, Health and Welfare Department, in Chapter XI.

Three Departments are common service Departments—Organisation and Establishments, Finance and Solicitor's—and the heads of these Departments are responsible directly to the Permanent Secretary. The services which they provide are the subject of the following chapter. The Chief Industrial Commissioner who is responsible for the Industrial Relations and Statistics Departments, also reports directly to the Permanent Secretary. The remaining seven Departments fall into two groups, for each of which a Deputy Secretary is responsible, subject to the overriding responsibility of the Permanent Secretary. One of the Ministry's Deputy Secretaries is also Chief International Labour Adviser to the Government, and in this capacity his experience and advice are available not only to the Ministry, but also to the Foreign Office, the Colonial Office and other Government Departments concerned in overseas labour questions.

Broad outlines of policy are discussed and formed at a level appropriate to the importance of the matter concerned; this may be at ministerial or senior official level. The work of implementing the policy, and of resolving minor policy questions arising from it, rests with the division. The work of divisions lends itself generally to organisation on a unitary or on a functional basis; in some cases both systems are adopted within the same division to deal with different types of work. The unitary system is usually practised where there is a constant flow of work more or less uniform in character (for example, individual cases needing to be dealt with) which requires the application of the same methods and criteria. The functional system is more appropriate when the work consists of dealing with policy developments which cannot be tackled by applying hard and fast principles and precedents laid down in advance. The charts on page 180 give examples of two divisions, one of which is organised on a unitary basis and the other on a functional basis. The work of a division is generally split into sections each of which is under the control of an executive officer of appropriate rank.

The Ministry also has a large regional and local organisation which is the subject of Chapter XVI. On matters of organisation and generally, regional controllers are responsible to the Director of Organisation and Establishments at the Ministry's Headquarters,

ORGANISATION ON A UNITARY BASIS OF A DIVISION OF OVERSEAS DEPARTMENT

Consideration of applications and the issue of permits under Article 4 (1) (b) of the Aliens Order, 1953: consideration of applications for permission to employ aliens already admitted to this country as visitors or students; extension of periods of permits, etc.

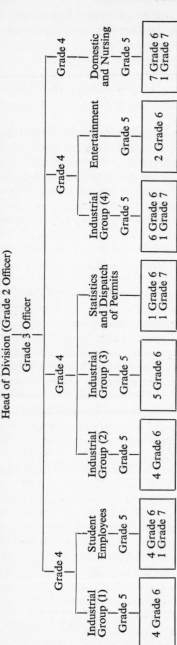

Head of Division (Grade 2 Officer)

Grade 3 Officer

	Grade 4			Grade 4		Grade 4		Grade 4
Industrial Group (1)	Student Employees		Industrial Group (2)	Industrial Group (3)	Statistics and Dispatch of Permits	Industrial Group (4)	Entertainment	Domestic and Nursing
Grade 5	Grade 5		Grade 5	Grade 5		Grade 5	Grade 5	Grade 5
4 Grade 6	4 Grade 6 / 1 Grade 7		4 Grade 6	5 Grade 6	1 Grade 6 / 1 Grade 7	6 Grade 6 / 1 Grade 7	2 Grade 6	7 Grade 6 / 1 Grade 7

ORGANISATION ON A FUNCTIONAL BASIS OF A DIVISION OF TRAINING DEPARTMENT

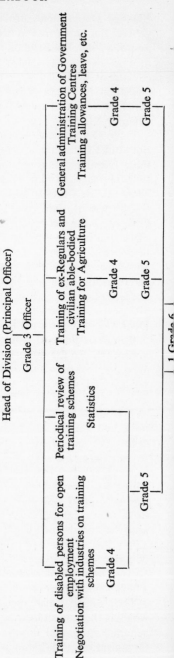

Head of Division (Principal Officer)

Grade 3 Officer

Training of disabled persons for open employment. Negotiation with industries on training schemes	Periodical review of training schemes. Statistics	Training of ex-Regulars and civilian able-bodied. Training for Agriculture	General administration of Government Training Centres. Training allowances, leave, etc.
Grade 4		Grade 4	Grade 4
Grade 5	Grade 5	Grade 5	Grade 5
	1 Grade 6		

but they obtain advice and guidance on matters related to specific functions of the Ministry by direct contact with the Headquarters Departments concerned.

Staffing of the Ministry

Excluding branch managers and local agents, the number of staff employed in the Ministry on 1st January, 1958, was 20,871, of whom 2,273 were in post at Headquarters.[1]

In common with other Government Departments the Ministry draws most of its staff from the Civil Service Commission's allocation of successful candidates from competitive examinations and interviews. New entrants come from the four main Civil Service competitions for the Administrative, Executive and Clerical Classes and for clerical assistants and typists. Most Government Departments adopt a standard grading of officers within these main Treasury Classes but apart from a small number of recruits from the Administrative competition, most of the new entrants to the Ministry become members of a special Departmental Class designed to meet the particular needs of the Department.

Originally, the special Departmental Class was employed only in the local and regional offices, and all the staff at Headquarters belonged to the Treasury Classes. During the Second World War there was a good deal of intermingling of officers of the different classes with considerable benefit on both sides. This showed the need for a simpler and more flexible grading system which would permit freer movement between Headquarters and the out-stationed offices. In 1947 there was a complete reorganisation to effect the amalgamation of all the Treasury Classes below the Administrative with the Departmental grades to form a new Departmental Class with seven gradings. The new gradings were kept broadly in line with the general Civil Service gradings.

In the main, new entrants come from the Clerical Officer examination and the Clerical Assistant examination and enter the two Clerical grades. In addition, a number of recruits to these basic grades are older persons who have already served in a temporary capacity. A small number of 'direct entrants' into the Junior Executive grade are taken from the Executive examination, although the majority of appointments to this grade are made by promotion. Vacancies at all other levels are filled by promotion from the grade below except for the grade of Cadet Officers. A limited number of these are recruited annually through the special Departmental Class examination, which is a joint competition for entry to the Ministry

[1] These figures include industrial and non-industrial staff; part-time staff are counted as half-units.

and to some other Departments, open to candidates with a University degree or equivalent academic qualifications.

At Headquarters officers in the most senior of the departmental grades—Grade 1—take charge of certain specialist blocks of work. Grade 2 Officers stationed at Headquarters are frequently in charge of divisions where the content of the work is largely of an executive type; for example, in the charts shown of a unitary and a functional division, the former is the responsibility of a Grade 2 Officer and the latter of a Principal Officer.

The Factory Inspectorate and the legal staff are two groups outside the Departmental or Administrative Classes. They are both recruited from open competitions conducted by the Civil Service Commission. Other 'specialists' who have been mentioned in previous chapters such as the Personnel Management Advisers and the scientific and technical staff of the Technical and Scientific Register are usually recruited directly by the Ministry—via its own Employment Service—on a temporary basis.

Temporary clerical staff are engaged as required to meet the fluctuations in the volume of work in local offices—and occasionally also at regional offices and Headquarters. At various periods in the Ministry's history—during the last war particularly and in times of heavy unemployment before it—this temporary 'fringe' has been large. Many of the officers who began in this way were eventually established and now form a considerable proportion of the permanent staff alongside the normal entrants by examination.

A carefully planned series of allocations to provide training on the job goes hand in hand with more direct methods of training for a new officer in the first five years of service to give him a varied and all-round experience of the work of the Ministry. Any attempt to specialise is discouraged during these years but later, as far as can be managed, an officer is increasingly given opportunity to follow his bent and spend longer periods on the type of work for which he is most fitted. Personal records of progressive allocations, experience obtained and training courses taken are maintained for each officer.

Premises

In common with other Government Departments with Headquarters in London, the Ministry has had to house its Headquarters staff in scattered premises. In 1941, 8 St James's Square replaced Montagu House, Whitehall, as the ministerial Headquarters of the Ministry. Most of the senior staff are stationed there. Many of the other Headquarters staff are dispersed among a number of buildings in the London area and some are as far away as Watford.

In the early stages of the Second World War the decrease in the volume of the work of the Ministry for the relief of unemployment, and the emphasis on its employment functions, led to a new approach to the planning and equipment of Employment Exchanges. The exchange premises taken over by the Board of Trade in 1909—mostly converted shops, offices and village halls—served their purpose reasonably well in the very early years of the service. They were inadequate, however, to cope with the heavy unemployment of the inter-war years and many makeshift premises were taken over to accommodate the large numbers claiming unemployment benefit. The more varied functions laid on the Ministry from the beginning of the last war and the reduction in unemployment increased the proportion of individual work requiring privacy and reduced the need for large open rooms. At the same time, the desire to provide pleasant informal rooms for private interviews could not be realised at the expense of having insufficient accommodation to deal with a sudden increase in the numbers unemployed. Since the war, with the co-operation of the Ministry of Works, the answer to these needs has been found in the use, for private interviews, of standard movable cubicles, which can be put up in large rooms and varied in number and location to suit current needs. Improved standards are being applied gradually as new exchanges are built or as an exchange moves to new premises.

This new equipment, aided by a more imaginative use of colour, is doing much to remove the institutional appearance of exchanges, which was for so long a source of criticism. No less important is the interest taken by the exchange manager and his staff in keeping the office tidy and cheerful and in displaying, in an attractive, imaginative and easily read form, a selection of the employment vacancies currently available. These improvements have been welcomed by the public, who appreciate the more attractive and comfortable conditions, and even more the increased privacy afforded in so many offices today.

CHAPTER XV

Common Services

*

THERE are three Headquarters common service Departments which serve the Ministry as a whole. These are the Organisation and Establishments Department, the Finance Department and the Solicitor's Department. Administrative divisions keep in close touch with these Departments on all relevant matters, and make use of their services as necessary. The work of these common service Departments is in many ways similar to that of their counterparts in other Government Departments, but it is, of course, specialised to the extent that it is related to matters within the ambit of the Ministry.

The Organisation and Establishments Department

This Department is responsible for the recruitment, allocation, control, welfare and training of the staff of the Ministry; for establishment, organisation and procedure questions, for accommodation and common services such as typing and messengerial facilities; for public relations, and for the control of work undertaken on an agency basis for other Government Departments. It undertakes consultation with the Treasury on all staff matters and negotiates with the Staff Side of the Departmental Whitley Council and with staff associations. It is controlled by an Under-Secretary with the functional title of Director of Organisation and Establishments and consists of four branches of which three are under the charge of Assistant Secretaries and the fourth under the Chief Information Officer.

Two branches of the Department deal with the broad group of issues which may be called personnel matters. These include all questions governing conditions of service (e.g. recruitment, rates of pay, hours of work, seniority, overtime, leave, welfare), staff estimates and records, the training of staff, promotions, superannuation, posting and all other matters relating to the maintenance and control of the whole of the Ministry's staff.

A third branch includes the Chief Inspector and the Chief Instructions Officer with their staffs, and also has the general responsibility for all matters relating to premises and accommodation, motor transport, travel services, printing, stores and stationery. It controls the registries,[1] typing services, messengers and cleaning services. The Chief Inspector is responsible for the carrying out of functional surveys concerned with the efficiency of methods of work and the organisation of the Ministry, and staffing surveys of Headquarters branches and regional offices; for advising on the best and most effective way in which proposed new items of work should be organised and on changes in procedure or other action which appear necessary for the effective performance of the Ministry's functions; and also for dealing with matters relating to occupational classification.

The Chief Instructions Officer is responsible, in consultation with the administrative divisions concerned, for advising on the procedure and methods to be adopted in carrying out items of work devolved to the regional organisation; for the design and control of forms; for the preparation and issue of all circular instructions to the staff; for the examination of proposals for new statistical returns and the review of existing returns; for dealing with suggestions by the staff for improving procedure; and for liaison with the Ministry of Pensions and National Insurance and the National Assistance Board on questions of procedure in carrying out the agency services undertaken for those Departments.

The responsibilities of the Chief Information Officer are fivefold: he seeks to promote public understanding of new measures and the reasons for them; to keep the public acquainted with the services available to them; to campaign for any special needs indicated by the administrative branches; to maintain a high standard in the quality of the printed material presented to the public; and to ensure that the views of the general public, as expressed in the Press and elsewhere, are brought to the notice of the Ministry. He maintains, therefore, close relations not only with all sections of the Ministry but also with the Press, the broadcasting authorities, the Central Office of Information, and the public relations officers of other Government Departments.

The Finance Department

All financial, accounting and audit questions affecting the Ministry are dealt with in the Finance Department. The Accountant-General, who is the Under-Secretary in charge of the Department, is the chief

---

[1] The functions of a registry are to receive and distribute all official correspondence, record and file particulars of all communications on official matters, collect and distribute papers between officers and Departments, keep a record of the movement of all registered papers and, when action is completed or suspended, file such papers for reference purposes.

financial adviser to the Permanent Secretary who, as 'Accounting Officer', is personally responsible to Parliament for the expenditure of the money voted annually for use by the Ministry and for the submission of the Ministry's annual appropriation account.

Two branches of the Department are concerned with financial policy and advise the administrative divisions on the financial effect of all proposals involving expenditure, with particular regard to the responsibility of the Accounting Officer for such expenditure and to its propriety in regard to Parliamentary and Treasury requirements. They obtain Treasury authority for expenditure other than that

	£
Administration (salaries, travelling expenses, law charges, etc.)	16,444,451
Adjudication, advisory services, etc.	64,809
Employment, transference, hostels, training and rehabilitation (includes grants to local authorities for the administration of the Youth Employment Service, costs of the National Institute of Houseworkers Ltd., etc.)	3,032,267
Special facilities for seriously disabled persons (grants to Remploy Ltd., local authorities, voluntary bodies etc.)	3,416,470
National Service	651,018
Other services (includes repayment of loan charges in respect of employment schemes, subscription to the International Labour Organisation, etc.)	862,508
Losses and compensation	3,063
Gross Total Expenditure	£24,474,586
Total Receipts	£3,720,109

relating to establishment questions. It is their duty to watch the course of expenditure and, in conjunction with the administrative divisions, to estimate the sums required to finance the various services of the Ministry. They also examine and prepare replies to questions raised by the Comptroller and Auditor General.

A third branch is responsible for all payments made from the Ministry's Headquarters, for the examination of monthly accounts from local offices, for internal audit and for central accounting including Parliamentary Votes and Estimates.

A fourth branch of Finance Department is responsible for the examination of the weekly benefit, etc., accounts of local offices and embraces the Regional Finance Officer stationed in each region. These officers work in close liaison with the Regional Controllers but are responsible to the Finance Department. They supervise the Ministry's financial and accounting arrangements in the region, make certain payments themselves, keep the Ministry's local offices in funds and undertake audit examinations of such offices.

The various accounts kept in the Ministry are brought together monthly and are used to build up the annual appropriation account which is submitted to the Comptroller and Auditor General and the Treasury for presentation to Parliament.

In 1956–57 the gross expenditure by the Ministry on its services, together with the administrative costs of agency services (mostly recoverable from other Government Departments) was made up as shown in the table on the previous page.

Certain other costs of the Ministry estimated at about £5,969,350 were borne by other Government Departments. Such services include rental values of premises, maintenance, furniture, fuel and light, rates, stationery and printing, postal services and superannuation. In addition to these sums the Ministry paid out about £30 million by way of social service benefits, etc., on behalf of other Government Departments.

The Solicitor's Department

The Solicitor's Department undertakes advisory work, civil litigation, prosecutions, conveyancing, the drafting of subordinate legislation and preparatory work in connection with Bills for the Ministry. The greater part of the advisory work relates to the interpretation of the various statutes for the administration of which the Minister is responsible, such as the Wages Councils Acts, the Factories Acts and the National Service Acts.

The Solicitor plays an important part when new legislation is under consideration in the Ministry, since inevitably many legal questions arise. When new legislative proposals have taken shape in the Ministry the Solicitor, in close co-operation with the administrative Departments concerned, prepares the instructions for the preparation of a Bill, which go from the Ministry to Parliamentary Counsel; and thereafter he forms the link between Parliamentary Counsel, who drafts the Bill, and the Ministry. He also advises on any legal questions that arise in the course of the Parliamentary proceedings on the Bill.

The Solicitor is responsible for the drafting of statutory instruments, i.e. orders, regulations, etc., made under the various statutes administered by the Ministry, and having the force of law. In addition to the technical drafting of the instruments it is his duty to ensure that the powers given by the statute are not exceeded. He also advises the Ministry on matters connected with the various international instruments with which the Ministry is concerned. This involves, for instance, questions relating to Conventions and Recommendations of the International Labour Organisation, dealing not only with the interpretation of these instruments but also with their ratification, having regard to the law in the United Kingdom.

Civil litigation and criminal prosecutions with which the Ministry is concerned are dealt with by the Solicitor's Department. On the civil side, for example, there are actions for the recovery of money owing to workers under the Wages Councils Acts or the Catering Wages Act, and the Ministry as a large employer has to deal from time to time with claims for damages in respect of accidents and injuries. In recent years there has been a steady flow of cases in the High Court relating to the powers and functions of the Industrial Disputes Tribunal which have been of importance in the field of industrial arbitration. On the criminal side there are prosecutions for offences under various Acts, such as the Wages Councils Acts and the National Service Acts. Prosecutions for Factories Acts offences, which are undertaken by factory inspectors in the Magistrates' Courts, are dealt with by the Solicitor when an appeal is involved—either to quarter sessions or by way of Case Stated to the High Court. The Solicitor also acts for Remploy Ltd., and the National Institute of Houseworkers Ltd. Most of the conveyancing work is in connection with Remploy Ltd.

The Solicitor's department consists of barristers and solicitors and a small clerical staff. Most of the actual litigation in Magistrates' Courts outside the London area is conducted on agency terms by local solicitors. Members of the staff conduct London cases when possible and also, because of their complexity, cases in England and Wales under the Catering Wages Act and the Wages Councils Acts. In the higher Courts the Ministry appears by counsel instructed by the Solicitor. Cases of first importance are taken by one of the Law Officers of the Crown. Criminal proceedings in Scotland are the concern of the Procurator Fiscal, although factory inspectors prosecute for Factories Acts offences, and in civil matters the Ministry acts through a solicitor in Scotland appointed by the Lord Advocate.

CHAPTER XVI

Regional and Local Organisation

*

THE nature of the work of the Ministry is such that much of it has been decentralised and is directed from nine[1] regional offices in England and offices in Scotland and Wales, each in the charge of a Controller who is of assistant secretary rank.[2] The regional boundaries conform, with one or two minor deviations, to the standard boundaries determined by the Government's Inter-Departmental Regional Organisation Committee. The regional offices have been modelled broadly on the pattern existing in the Ministry's Headquarters, and their organisation has developed on parallel lines to that at Headquarters as the responsibilities and functions of the Ministry have changed. The organisation of a typical regional office is shown in Chart I, Appendix I.

Regional offices carry out industrial relations work, ensure compliance with Orders made under the Wages Councils Acts and the Catering Wages Acts, and for the call-up of men registered under the National Service Acts. They are also responsible for the control and efficiency of the work performed at the Ministry's local offices, Government Training Centres and industrial rehabilitation units. The work of the regional offices in the sphere of industrial relations is of great importance, and has been referred to in Chapter VIII of this book. Regional Industrial Relations Officers are stationed in each regional office and keep the Department in touch with local developments likely to result in trade disputes. Each of these officers has on his staff conciliation officers who are at the service of employers and workpeople when differences arise which the parties concerned find difficulty in settling. The Regional Industrial Relations Officer may himself act as a conciliation officer in the more difficult cases, and this work of the regional offices is of great assistance in helping to maintain good industrial relations throughout the country. A

[1] Reduced to eight in 1958.
[2] In the remainder of this chapter 'region', 'regional office' and 'Regional Controller' are used as convenient general terms to include Scotland and Wales and the offices and Controllers for Scotland and Wales, the former of which are termed individually 'Scottish Headquarters' and 'Wales Office'.

number of inter-departmental committees[1] also function on a regional basis and carry a responsibility which would otherwise be borne at Headquarters.

The smooth functioning of a large organisation is naturally largely dependent on close working relationships within the organisation. Within the Ministry there are arrangements for ensuring co-operation and understanding between Headquarters, regional and local staff. Apart from the constant day-to-day contacts between them by way of correspondence, telephone or personal visit arising from the work, there are meetings at regular intervals for the discussion of problems and the interchange of ideas. Each month Regional Controllers attend a conference at the Headquarters of the Ministry, of which the Permanent Secretary is Chairman, at which current problems and proposals for future action are discussed with the senior administrative staff. Regional Controllers have regular meetings with their senior Employment Exchange managers with a similar purpose, at which the Regional Controller can explain proposals emanating from Headquarters and obtain the views of local office[2] staff. These senior Employment Exchange managers in turn hold meetings with other exchange managers in their area, and a complete channel of communication, going beyond formal instruction and working in either direction, thus extends from Permanent Secretary to Employment Exchange manager. In addition, specialised conferences dealing, for example, with industrial relations, vocational training and the problems of the disabled, are held periodically, both at Headquarters and regional offices.

Local Organisation

The bulk of the executive work of the Ministry is carried out in its local offices. There is at least one Employment Exchange in every town of any size, and there are several in each of the large industrial centres. Many of them have sub-offices or part-time offices in other parts of their areas. Employment Exchanges are of four grades, each being controlled by a manager of corresponding grade, i.e. a Grade 2, Grade 3, Grade 4 or Grade 5 Officer, as appropriate. The grading varies broadly according to the volume of work but the nature of local contacts is also taken into consideration. The difference in

---

[1] Inter-departmental regional committees attended are: Regional Civil Defence Co-ordinating Committee, Regional Board for Industry, Regional Building Committee, Regional Physical Planning Committee, Regional Distribution of Industry Panel, Building and Civil Engineering Regional Joint Committee, Regional Emergency Committee.

[2] 'Local office' is the term used within the Ministry to refer to all the Employment Exchanges and sub-offices, part-time offices, branch employment offices and local agencies.

size and number of staff between the largest office with some 200 staff and the smallest offices with only two or three staff results in many variations of organisation (see Charts 2–4, Appendix I).

Branch employment offices are attached to some Employment Exchanges to serve country districts or small market towns. The branch office managers are not civil servants but contract as agents of the Ministry to carry out most of the duties of an Employment Exchange. There are also 'local agencies' attached to some Employment Exchanges to serve some of the most isolated rural districts and these, too, are run on a contractual basis; they have very limited functions related mainly to applications for unemployment benefit or National Assistance and registration for National Service.

The work done by the Employment Exchange service includes many other duties in addition to those which the public usually associate with Employment Exchanges. The offices exist primarily to place men and women in the employment for which they are most suited, but their other duties generally include the special service for disabled persons; the submission of suitable candidates for vocational training or rehabilitation courses; registration for National Service; advising and helping on problems of workers' welfare and making payments such as lodging allowances to transferred workers; preparing statistical returns and reports; and undertaking local work for other Government Departments including that in connection with claims for unemployment benefit and assistance.

The greater part of the work of the Employment Exchanges has been dealt with item by item in Part II of this book and especially in the chapter dealing with the employment service, but the work undertaken as an agency service for other Government Departments has not been described. The objects of arranging for one Government Department with a well-established local service to undertake local services for another are to provide a more efficient service to the public and to effect economies in public expenditure. The proposal to initiate a new agency scheme may come from a variety of quarters, but its practicability is usually examined jointly by the organisation and methods officers of the Government Departments concerned, who may then proceed by way of experiment. When the main procedures have been agreed, the Instructions Branch prepares the necessary instructions. The Finance Departments of the Ministries concerned decide the manner in which repayment of costs of the service shall be made. Policy matters and the responsibility to Parliament for such matters remain with the Government Department for whom the service is rendered, but questions raised in Parliament in connection with the day-to-day administration of the agency service are answered by the Minister of the Agency Department.

The main agency services at present undertaken by the Ministry are the payment of unemployment benefit and National Assistance to unemployed persons on behalf of the Ministry of Pensions and National Insurance and the National Assistance Board, respectively; work in connection with the issue of passports on behalf of the Foreign Office; and work performed for the Ministry of Health and the Department of Health for Scotland in connection with the cheap or free milk scheme.

Agency Services for the Ministry of Pensions and National Insurance and the National Assistance Board

Work in connection with the payment of unemployment benefit on behalf of the Ministry of Pensions and National Insurance is a continuation of a function for which the Ministry once had sole responsibility. When, in 1945, the control of unemployment insurance was transferred from the Ministry to the new Ministry of National Insurance, it was realised that it would be necessary to maintain the same close link as previously between registration for employment and the claiming of unemployment benefit. It is not only in the claimant's interest that these should be closely linked; it is also essential to the administration of the National Insurance Act, which makes 'availability for work' a condition of entitlement to benefit. The payment of benefit was therefore left with the Ministry, but on an agency basis. For similar reasons, the Ministry continues to pay assistance to able-bodied unemployed applicants as agent for the National Assistance Board.

The work carried out by Employment Exchanges and youth employment offices in connection with unemployment benefit involves taking claims for benefit, obtaining proof of unemployment, considering each claimant's entitlement to benefit, and making the appropriate payments. In addition, credits of National Insurance contributions are granted as appropriate to unemployed persons. Youth employment offices also undertake the issue of National Insurance cards to boys and girls under the age of 18 who are taking up employment for the first time.

The National Insurance Acts provide that all claims for benefit are to be submitted, in the first instance, to Insurance Officers who are appointed under the Acts. Certain officers in the Ministry's regional and local offices have been appointed as Insurance Officers by the Ministry of Pensions and National Insurance, and these officers either decide for or against claimants for unemployment benefit or refer the claim for decision by a Local Tribunal. Questions in connection with claims for unemployment benefit which may have to be decided include whether the claimant is available for employment, whether he has refused suitable employment or has left employment voluntarily without good cause. Questions on which the Insurance Officer is not prepared to give a decision and appeals made against disallowance are referred to a local tribunal set up by the Ministry of Pensions and National Insurance. Each tribunal consists of a Chairman (usually, but not always, a lawyer) and two members, one drawn from a panel representing employers and one from a panel representing employed persons. In certain cases, an appeal may be made against the decision of the local tribunal to the National Insurance Commissioner, an independent statutory authority appointed by the Crown, whose decision is final. There is no similar formal procedure for National Assistance cases; if an applicant for National Assistance refuses employment or seems to be failing to take advantage of opportunities for employment, the local office notifies the area office of the National Assistance Board.

There is little need for direct contact between the local offices of the two Ministries, except in cases of consecutive periods of sickness and unemployment. Local offices of the Ministry of Labour and National Service apply directly to the records branch of the Ministry of Pensions and National Insurance at Newcastle upon Tyne for details of the contribution record of each person making a claim for unemployment benefit; this record governs the duration and rate of benefit.

Repayments of income tax to taxpayers who are unemployed and who have had deducted from wages an amount greater in the aggregate than the cumulative tax due are made by local offices of the Ministry. These repayments are made under arrangements agreed between the Ministry and the Board of Inland Revenue in April, 1944, when the system of collection of income tax by weekly deductions from wages was introduced.

Agency Service for the Passport Office of the Foreign Office

Since April, 1947, the Ministry has provided a local service for people wishing to obtain, or to renew, or to have additional particulars endorsed on, a United Kingdom passport.

The Ministry's officers do not issue passports, but only the application forms. They give advice on the filling up of the forms, accept them when completed for despatch to the Passport Office, and collect the fees. The Passport Office determines whether the applicant is entitled to hold a passport, and its authorisation, preparation and issue rest with that Office.

The advantage of decentralising part of the work in this way is that the completed forms can be examined locally and queries dealt

N

with at the time of application, thus obviating correspondence between the applicant and the Passport Office and saving both time and labour. In addition, the supporting documents which have to be produced when an application is made can be examined locally and handed back to the applicant. Between the date of commencement of the agency service and the end of 1957, more than 3,400,000 passport applications have been dealt with at the Ministry's local offices. Members of the public who prefer to do so may still apply direct to the Passport Office or to a travel agency.

Agency Service for the Health Departments

The agency work for the Health Departments is undertaken at about 700 of the Ministry's local offices but is small in volume. It consists of counting and checking milk tokens for cheap or free milk received from milk retailers, and issuing certificates to the retailers which they present to a Milk Marketing Board for payment.

Local Co-operation with other Government Departments and Advisory Bodies

Certain local offices of the Ministry, mainly in smaller towns and rural areas, provide 'caller station' facilities for both the Ministry of Pensions and National Insurance and the National Assistance Board. This means that office accommodation on one or two days a week is made available to officers of these Departments in order that they may carry out their normal service to the public in the area. When officers from the Ministry of Pensions and National Insurance or the National Assistance Board are not in attendance at their caller stations, the staff of the local office of the Ministry have authority to perform certain of their duties, e.g. the issue of leaflets and dealing with routine inquiries.

Each Employment Exchange or group of exchanges is assisted by Advisory Committees which help to keep the Employment Exchange manager in touch with the views of employers and workpeople in his area and to secure for him the full benefit of local knowledge in all matters with which is he concerned. There is usually a Local Employment Committee and a Disablement Advisory Committee and, where the Youth Employment Service is administered by the Ministry, a Youth Employment Committee. These have a tripartite membership comprising an employers' panel, a workers' panel and an additional members' panel. The Chairman is appointed by the Minister. Many Local Employment Committees have a women's sub-committee, to deal with matters within their terms of reference particularly affecting women, whose constitution follows the pattern of the main Committee.

The efficiency of the regional and local organisation of the Ministry is of the greatest importance. The great majority of the public deal with the Ministry at its local offices, and it is therefore upon the service given in those offices that the efficiency of the Ministry is inevitably largely judged. It is the local staff who have the tasks of giving good service, day in and day out, to the local community and of resolving, equitably and courteously, the many difficult human problems with which they are faced. The principles laid down for their guidance, and the instructions, training and inspiration given them by the Ministry's Headquarters and regional offices are of the greatest importance, but human problems frequently fail to conform precisely with the circumstances envisaged in even the most widely drawn instructions. It therefore falls to the local staff to give satisfaction to all of those who avail themselves of the services of the Ministry, whether employers or workers or others, by giving effect to the Ministry's policy, not slavishly or mechanically, but with intelligence, understanding and humanity.

PART VII

In Retrospect

CHAPTER XVII

In Retrospect

*

IN looking back over the years since the formation of the Ministry of Labour towards the end of 1916, one is very conscious of the great changes that have taken place in its functions and duties and the differing emphasis that has been placed from time to time on various aspects of its work due to changing economic circumstances of the country and to the Second World War. Today the boundaries of its competence and activities extend far beyond the limits originally conceived; it has added to its former duties functions connected with such important matters as the calling up of men for National Service, the training, industrial rehabilitation and placing in employment of disabled persons, the safety, health and welfare of workpeople in factories, and international labour affairs including the labour aspects of work of the United Nations, the International Labour Organisation and other international agencies. But forming the centre of its activities and around which have been built its other functions and duties, there have remained throughout the industrial relations work and the work of the Employment Exchanges.

The early years of the Ministry were far from encouraging. As is said in the first chapter, the Ministry was born in a crisis and went from one crisis to another. It seems strange now to think that in the early 1920's there was a possibility of its abolition. Before it was firmly established it was called upon to deal with two problems of great difficulty—grave industrial unrest and serious unemployment. These problems were made all the more difficult to handle because hundreds of thousands of men returning from the First World War were expecting to come home to a land of prosperity and improved standards of life—'a land fit for heroes to live in'.

Serious disputes occurred in many industries and the resources of the Department, reinforced though they were by its new powers under the Industrial Courts Act, 1919, were taxed to the utmost. The mood of the workpeople was such that industrial unrest mounted progressively until it finally culminated in the general strike of 1926. At the same time the Department was called upon to endeavour to find work for the increasing numbers of unemployed and the

Employment Exchanges had to undertake the duty of paying them the 'out-of-work donation' each week. This was an overwhelming task for the exchanges which were ill-equipped and often housed in inadequate and sometimes deplorable premises. The out-of-work donation was commonly called 'the dole' and the exchanges were unable to escape some of the odium attaching to that expression. Even when a comprehensive measure of unemployment insurance was introduced and the unemployed were paid unemployment benefit to which they were entitled by virtue of the contributions they had paid, the payment was still regarded as the dole and this conception has never been completely eradicated. The exchanges, which had originally been set up before the 1914–18 war for the purpose of placing men in need of a job in touch with employers requiring labour, had little opportunity during these early years of the existence of the Ministry of carrying out their proper function. They were completely overwhelmed with the signing-on of the un-employed and with the payment of benefit. In fact, as one of the conditions for the receipt of benefit was that a man must be 'genuinely seeking work', men had to satisfy the exchange that they themselves had made efforts each week to secure work—it was not sufficient to come to the exchange and ask the latter to find employ-ment for them. It was not until well into the 1930's, when unemployment had decreased substantially and the great burden of unemployment insurance work was lifted to some extent, that the exchanges were once again able to devote some of their time to their proper work of placing people in employment.

It was during these years of mass unemployment, when the great majority of the exchanges had to sign on and pay tens of thousands of men and women each week, that the Ministry learned how to handle large numbers of people. The signing-on of and the payment of benefit to some thousands of workers at an exchange needed most careful organisation if chaos was to be avoided, and the experience which the staff gained at this time was to stand them in good stead when they were called upon in the war to register, call-up and allocate men and women for military service and for industrial mobilisation—it is hardly surprising that the staff felt that there was no task they could be given which they could not undertake. At the same time there was growing up in the Headquarters of the Ministry an administrative staff whose ability, developed and tempered by their experience of the massive problems with which they were required to deal, can be judged by the fact that after the Second World War no less than 10 of them became Permanent Secretaries, or their equivalent, of Departments in Whitehall—an outstanding record.

With the possibility of war, new tasks were placed on the Ministry —first of all the National Service campaign of 1938–39 and then the calling up of men for military training. These constructive tasks which brought the Ministry into completely new fields and faced them with fresh, and sometimes unusual, problems, were entered into with enthusiasm. The Military Training Act, involving as it did questions of conscientious objection and personal hardship in addition to the medical examination and calling up of large numbers of young men, brought out both the organisational powers of the staff and their humanitarian qualities. The Act itself was an outstanding piece of legislation which has stood the test of time in connection with such difficult issues as conscientious objection. For this, the country owes a debt of gratitude to the then Minister, Mr Ernest Brown, who became the first to hold the title of Minister of Labour and National Service.

It was during the war that the Ministry reached its zenith. It was given the task of mobilising the manpower of the nation, both military and civil, and the whole of its energy and its resources were devoted to that end. The Department was fortunate in having as its war minister Mr Ernest Bevin, a man of great knowledge and experience of labour matters and a man of purpose, drive and vision. Under his guidance the functions of the Department were expanded, notably in the safety, health and welfare field, and its powers greatly extended. The peak of manpower mobilisation was reached by September, 1943. It has been said, and it is almost certainly true, that the country's manpower was mobilised to a higher degree than any other nation in the world. What is undoubtedly true is that no country applied total mobilisation with greater humanity, none with greater regard for the personal circumstances and difficulties of the individual, none with greater fairness between individuals. In this the Ministry was greatly helped by the co-operation of all classes of the community—they were all anxious to help in the war effort. This was of enormous assistance to the Ministry as it meant that it was only in a comparatively few cases that the drastic power of directing people to take jobs had to be used.

The Employment Exchange machine was made a very flexible instrument concentrating at one time on manpower for the Forces, at another on manpower for munitions and, as required, on manpower for particular industries or services. The managers of the exchanges were given a latitude they had never enjoyed before. The Minister met all of them at a series of meetings throughout the country and told them that if something had to be done quickly, they were to do it without waiting for instructions from Headquarters as to how to do it. 'Use your heads', he said, 'and do what you think is right. I will back you, even if you make mistakes, provided you take action when you know it is needed.' Nothing more was required to maintain the morale of the staff at its highest level than instructions like this direct from Ernest Bevin.

In connection with the work of the exchanges it is perhaps appropriate to quote from a statement made by the then President of the Board of Trade (Mr, now Sir, Winston Churchill), in February, 1910, on the day that a large number of exchanges were first opened:

> 'They [i.e. the exchanges] are a piece of social mechanism, and are, I believe, absolutely essential to any well-ordered community. I am confident that 15 or 20 years hence people will as soon think of doing without a telephone exchange as without any system of labour bureaux. The success of Labour Exchanges will depend on the strict impartiality of the administration between capital and labour, between employers and workpeople. . . . They are primarily agencies for dealing with employment rather than with unemployment."

That conception of the work of the exchanges is as appropriate today as it was in 1910. Ernest Bevin had an even wider conception. Recognising that their work depended essentially on the maintenance of close contact with the community they served, he went so far as to regard it as essential that the exchanges should be built into the social fabric of the country.

After the war the Ministry entered upon its task of military and industrial demobilisation in the same spirit as it had carried out the mobilisation of the country's manpower. The plans, most carefully prepared during the war, worked extremely smoothly and military demobilisation and the reabsorption of ex-Servicemen and women in civilian life was completed by the end of 1947, while a few months later the re-allocation of industrial manpower had also been completed. And all this was achieved with practically no increase in unemployment. It was during this period that the Employment Exchanges began once again, as their major task, to perform their proper job of placing people in employment. Thus the Employment Exchange service has, since the formation of the Ministry, passed from the stage of being a national placing organisation to an agency for paying unemployment benefit, then to being the main instrument for mobilising the manpower of the country and subsequently demobilising it, and finally back to its proper function.

In addition to its main duties in the field of employment, the Ministry has had to carry out a number of tasks affecting particular classes of people. Two of the most important of these have been the vocational guidance and placing in employment of young persons, and the industrial rehabilitation, training and employment of disabled persons. There is nothing of greater importance to the future of the country than securing the most suitable and satisfying employment for our youth, and there is no more humanitarian task than rehabilitating the disabled and enabling them to take their place in the normal life of the community. The Department was fortunate to have the late Mr George Tomlinson as Parliamentary Secretary during the war, for it was he who, under the inspiration and guidance of Ernest Bevin, was responsible for the first scheme for the training and re-settlement into work of disabled persons. There is no doubt that the work upon which a person is engaged can have a considerable influence on his outlook and it has been evident in the Department that the work in connection with youth employment and with the industrial rehabilitation and employment of the disabled has brought out the best in the staff engaged on it. Many of those employed on both the youth and the disabled persons services have in fact become dedicated to their jobs. Of the Disabled Persons (Employment) Act, an observer has said: "As a piece of social planning the Act is almost flawless. It could have been conceived only by those who know that people matter more than things."[1] In the comprehensiveness of its provision for the disabled and in the integration of the many services involved, Great Britain holds a leading place in the world.

The work of the Ministry which is most in the public eye is that concerned with industrial relations. It is the threat of a stoppage of work, the actual strike or lock-out, and, to a lesser degree, the settlement of the dispute, that get the headlines. Of course, trade disputes and their settlement are of much importance to the prosperity of the country, but it is in the unobtrusive, day-to-day work in building up negotiating machinery and constitutional arrangements in industry for settling disputes, and in the advice given to employers and trade unions in the early stages of disputes that the Department accomplishes its most valuable work. Even in the period of acute industrial unrest following the First World War the Ministry was engaged in assisting in the establishment of Joint Industrial Councils—in fact, over 100 such Councils were formed although nearly half of them failed to survive the general strike in 1926. By the beginning of the Second World War the constant work of the Department, combined with the increasing growth and responsibility of the employers' associations and the trade unions, had resulted in most industries having negotiating machinery of their own for determining wages and conditions of employment and

1 See page 91.

constitutional arrangements for settling disputes. Further progress in this direction has been made since the end of the war.

A new problem has arisen in the last few years. The Nationalised Industries are required by statute to set up machinery for negotiating wages and conditions and for settling disputes, and in fact such machinery has been established and operated. It might be thought that in Nationalised Industries this should ensure industrial peace, but in practice this has not been the case. Owing to their failure to satisfy the workers in the industry, the decisions reached through the negotiating machinery have not always been accepted. In some cases the decision has been circumscribed by the inability of the industry to pay more without incurring additional losses. This has raised the question of the position of the Government as representing the State, the ultimate employer. Should the Government give instructions to the Nationalised Board as to the amount they should offer in connection with a claim for increased wages? If so, should the Government find the additional money, and would they not be liable to become involved themselves in negotiations with the unions? There is a further issue in connection with Nationalised Industries. No one denies the right of an individual to withhold his labour, but the view has certainly been growing that strikes and lock-outs are an outmoded—even barbarous—method of settling disputes. And this is very specially so in the case of Nationalised Industries, particularly if they are making losses instead of profits, as strike action injures the community in general and not a private employer.

These are current problems—problems of considerable importance to our industrial relations system—which could have the effect, if no satisfactory solution is evolved, of undermining the policy of self-government in industry so far as the determination of wages and conditions is concerned, a policy which has been followed by successive governments in this country for over half a century and which has resulted in our industrial relations system being the admiration of the world.

One of the outstanding features in the industrial scene since the end of the First World War has been the growth of employers' organisations and trade unions, and particularly the increased power of the trade unions. This increased power has brought with it increased responsibilities, responsibilities which have been specially evident during the years of full employment since the Second World War. The primary responsibility of a trade union is, of course, to its members, but at the same time, with the development of its power, the trade union movement has a responsibility to the community, a responsibility of which it has shown itself to be increasingly conscious with the rise in its power. It cannot, however, be said that the individual members of trade unions have recognised their responsibilities to the same extent, as is evidenced by the substantial number of 'unofficial' strikes. This again is a current problem of which the unions are fully conscious.

While there has been a gradual development both in the industrial relations system and in the part played by the Ministry, a more rapid development has taken place in recent years in human relations. There has been a much greater recognition of the importance of the human factor in industry, and the combined work of the Industrial Relations Department and the Safety, Health and Welfare Department of the Ministry, together with the co-operation of the voluntary associations, has enabled advice and assistance to be given to industry on an increasing scale.

It is natural that in looking back over the 40 years since the formation of the Ministry the main stress should be laid on the continuous and continuing work of industrial relations and of the Employment Exchanges. But at the same time emphasis must be given to the fact that, since the end of the Second World War, the duties of the Ministry in the international labour and in the safety, health and welfare fields have assumed increasing importance and have affected the balance of its functions.

Since 1945 there has been a series of economic crises as a result of an adverse external trade balance, with its effect on the stability of the pound, and of internal inflationary pressure. As a consequence, the necessity to increase productivity in order to secure economic stability has been fully recognised, and many measures have been taken for this purpose. The removal of impediments to production has assumed particular importance and one result has been a greater appreciation of the value of safety and industrial health measures in factories in order to make the maximum use of the labour employed. At the same time the growing recognition of the importance of the human factor in industry, to which reference has already been made, has led to more attention being given to providing good working conditions. These two factors—recognition of the need to provide better working conditions as a contribution to human happiness and the emergence of increased productivity as vital to the country's economic future—have therefore caused considerably greater value to be attached to the safety, health and welfare work of the Ministry. In addition, the scope of this work has in recent years been widened as a result of the new hazards, some of them of a dangerous nature, arising from the rapid developments taking place, particularly in the electronic and atomic fields.

At the end of the First World War the International Labour

Organisation was established for the purpose of helping to secure the permanent peace of the world by the establishment of social justice through an improvement of conditions of labour. Since the end of the Second World War, with the growth of tension between nations arising from the 'cold war' and the upsurge of nationalism, and with the increasing influence which labour is exercising on general policy in all countries, the securing of improved labour standards in the more backward countries, and thus the work of the International Labour Organisation, have become of paramount importance. One of the factors in obtaining such an improvement is the exchange of information on labour matters between nations leading to a greater knowledge of each other's methods and outlook, to a better appreciation and understanding of each other's point of view, and to the creation of mutual goodwill. In this the appointment of Labour Attachés has enabled invaluable service to be given both to this country and to the countries in which they work. The United Kingdom has always exercised great influence in the counsels of the International Labour Organisation. With the establishment of the United Nations and the other Specialised Agencies associated with it, and with the expansion of the scope and content of the work of the International Labour Organisation, the responsibilities falling on the Ministry have greatly increased and the sphere of influence of this country in labour matters has greatly extended.

It is too close in time to assess the value of the services of the Ministry to the country during the 40 years of its existence. While it is essentially an industrial Department, some of its activities are of a social nature and have had an impact on recent social history. In its earlier days there can be little doubt that it made some contribution to the problems of employment and the relief of unemployment and helped to establish on a firm footing arrangements in industry which led to a measure of industrial peace. In the Second World War the extent of the national war effort was conditioned by the manpower available and by mobilising the manpower of the country to the maximum it has been universally recognised that the Ministry made a contribution of outstanding value to the country. A similar contribution resulted from the effective military and industrial demobilisation that was carried out in the two years after the war.

This is a retrospect and it is not therefore permissible to look into the future, but, based on the experience of the last 40 years, this much can be said with confidence, that whatever task the Ministry is called upon to perform it will not be deterred by any difficulties or complexities but will enter into it with a determination to carry it through to a successful conclusion.

APPENDIX I

CHART 1
ORGANISATION OF A TYPICAL REGIONAL OFFICE OF THE MINISTRY OF LABOUR AND NATIONAL SERVICE

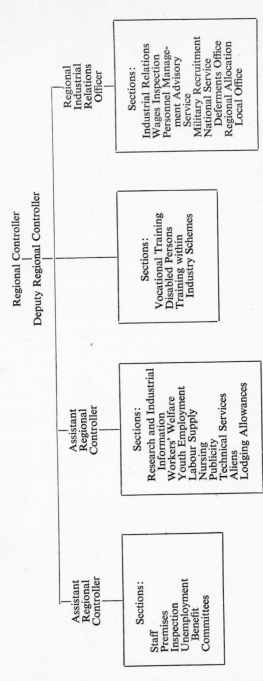

Regional Controller

Deputy Regional Controller

Assistant Regional Controller

Assistant Regional Controller

Regional Industrial Relations Officer

Sections:

Staff
Premises
Inspection
Unemployment
Benefit
Committees

Sections:

Research and Industrial
Information
Workers' Welfare
Youth Employment
Labour Supply
Nursing
Publicity
Technical Services
Aliens
Lodging Allowances

Sections:

Vocational Training
Disabled Persons
Training within
Industry Schemes

Sections:

Industrial Relations
Wages Inspection
Personnel Management Advisory
Service
Military Recruitment
National Service
Deferments Office
Regional Allocation
Local Office

NOTE 1: Regional Controllers are of assistant secretary rank, Deputy Regional Controllers of Grade 1 rank and Assistant Regional Controllers of Grade 2 rank. Regional Industrial Relations Officers and Heads of Sections are generally Grade 2 and Grade 3 respectively.
NOTE 2: The grouping of the Sections for which Assistant Regional Controllers are responsible varies in accordance with the particular needs of different regions. The number of Assistant Regional Controllers also varies, and the Deputy Regional Controller does not have direct sectional responsibilities in the larger regions.

CHART 2

ORGANISATION OF A SMALL EMPLOYMENT EXCHANGE

Manager (Grade 5 Officer)

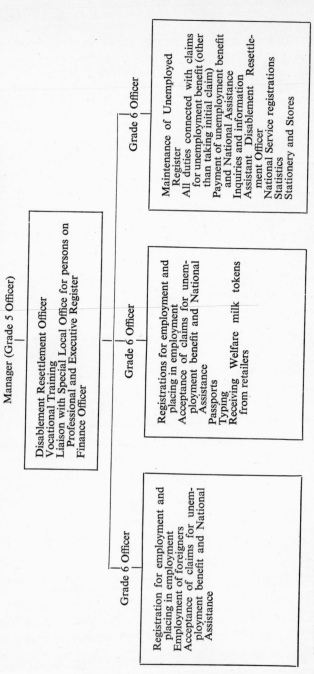

Disablement Resettlement Officer
Vocational Training
Liaison with Special Local Office for persons on Professional and Executive Register
Finance Officer

Grade 6 Officer

Registration for employment and placing in employment
Employment of foreigners
Acceptance of claims for unemployment benefit and National Assistance

Grade 6 Officer

Registrations for employment and placing in employment
Acceptance of claims for unemployment benefit and National Assistance
Passports
Typing
Receiving Welfare milk tokens from retailers

Grade 6 Officer

Maintenance of Unemployed Register
All duties connected with claims for unemployment benefit (other than taking initial claim)
Payment of unemployment benefit and National Assistance
Inquiries and information
Assistant Disablement Resettlement Officer
National Service registrations
Statistics
Stationery and Stores

NOTE: At offices with eight or less staff, all public business is where possible carried out in one room with separate provision for private interviews.

CHART 3

ORGANISATION OF A MEDIUM-SIZED EMPLOYMENT EXCHANGE

Manager (Grade 4 Officer)

Secretary of Local Employment Committee
Secretary of Disablement Advisory Committee
Liaison with Special Local Office for persons on
Professional and Executive Register
Local Insurance Officer

Employment and Disablement Resettlement

Grade 5 Officer

Registrations for employment and placing in employment
Vocational training
Disablement Resettlement Officer
Placing and follow-up of disabled persons
Maintenance of Disabled Persons Register
Quota scheme inspections
National Service registrations
Employment of foreigners
Receiving Welfare milk tokens from retailers
Acceptance of claims for unemployment benefit and National Assistance
Statistics (part)

Unemployment Benefit and Common Services

Grade 5 Officer

Maintenance of Unemployed Register
All duties connected with claims for unemployment benefit (other than taking initial claim)
Payment of unemployment benefit and National Assistance
Passports
Inquiries and Information
Finance Officer
Premises
Staff Records
Stationery and Stores
Post
Typing
Telephone switchboard
Statistics (part)

The clerical staff consists of:—

8 Grade 6 Officers
2 Grade 7 Officers
1 Shorthand Typist

NOTE: Men and women are normally dealt with together in all Departments.

CHART 4

ORGANISATION OF A LARGE EMPLOYMENT EXCHANGE

Manager (Grade 3 Officer)

Secretary of Local Employment Committee

Deputy Manager (Grade 4 Officer)

Men's Employment Section 1	Men's Employment Section 2	Men's Disablement Resettlement Section	Women's Employment and Disablement Resettlement Section	Unemployment Benefit Section (Men and Women combined).	Adjudication Section	Common Services
Grade 5 Officer	Grade 5 Officer	Grade 5 Officer	Grade 5 Officer	Grade 5 Officer	Grade 5 Officer	Grade 5 Officer
Registrations for employment and placing in employment in building trades, coalmining, agriculture and engineering Acceptance of claims for unemployment benefit and National Assistance Vocational training	Registrations for employment and placing in employment in commercial occupations and miscellaneous trades Acceptance of claims for unemployment benefit and National Assistance Employment of foreigners Liaison with Special Local Office for persons on Professional and Executive Register	Disablement Resettlement Officer Secretary, Disablement Advisory Committee Placing and follow-up of disabled persons Maintenance of Disabled Persons Register Quota scheme inspection	Registrations for employment and placing in employment Vocational training of foreigners Employment of foreigners Acceptance of claims for unemployment benefit and National Assistance Disablement Resettlement Officer Placing and follow-up of disabled persons Maintenance of Disabled Persons Register Secretary, Women's Sub-Committee of Local Employment Committee	Maintenance of Unemployed Register All duties connected with claims to unemployment benefit (other than taking initial claim) Payment of unemployment benefit and National Assistance National Service registrations	Local Insurance Officer Decisions on questions of doubt on claims to unemployment benefit in own and neighbouring offices	Finance Officer Staff Records Premises Post Telephone Switchboard Typing Statistics Inquiries and information Service Receiving Welfare milk tokens from retailers Passports Stationery and stores

The clerical staff consists of: 23 Grade 6 Officers, 6 Grade 7 Officers, 1 Telephone Operator, 1 Shorthand Typist, 1 Messenger.

MINISTERS OF LABOUR AND PERIOD OF OFFICE, 1916–56

December, 1916–August, 1917	Rt. Hon. John Hodge, M.P.
August, 1917–November, 1918	Rt. Hon. G. H. Roberts, M.P.
November, 1918–February, 1920	Rt. Hon. Sir R. Horne, M.P.
February, 1920–October, 1922	Rt. Hon. T. J. Macnamara, M.P.
October, 1922–January, 1924	Rt. Hon. Sir Montague Barlow, M.P.
January, 1924–November, 1924	Rt. Hon. Tom Shaw, M.P.
November, 1924–May, 1929	Rt. Hon. Sir Arthur Steel-Maitland, M.P.
June, 1929–August, 1931	Rt. Hon. Margaret Bondfield, M.P.
August, 1931–June, 1934	Rt. Hon. Sir Henry Betterton, M.P.
July, 1934–June, 1935	Rt. Hon. Oliver Stanley, M.P.
June, 1935–May, 1940	Rt. Hon. Ernest Brown, M.P.
May, 1940–May, 1945	Rt. Hon. Ernest Bevin, M.P.
May, 1945–July, 1945	Rt. Hon. R. A. Butler, M.P.
July, 1945–17th January, 1951	Rt. Hon. G. A. Isaacs, M.P.
18th January, 1951–23rd April, 1951	Rt. Hon. Aneurin Bevan, M.P.
24th April, 1951–25th October, 1951	Rt. Hon. A. Robens, M.P.
26th October, 1951–20th December, 1955	Rt. Hon. Sir Walter Monckton, M.P.
21st December, 1955	Rt. Hon. Iain Macleod, M.P.

PERMANENT SECRETARIES, 1916–56

15th December, 1916–29th August, 1921	Sir David Shackleton, K.C.B.
30th August, 1921–16th November, 1930	Sir Horace Wilson, K.C.B., C.B.E.
17th November, 1930–8th January, 1935	Sir Francis Floud, K.C.B.
9th January, 1935–17th November, 1944	Sir Thomas Phillips, K.C.B., K.B.E.
18th November, 1944–31st January, 1956	Sir Godfrey Ince, G.C.B., K.B.E.
1st February, 1956	Sir Harold Emmerson, G.C.B., K.C.V.O.

Index

Advisory Council on the Relationship between Employment in the Services and Civilian Life, 16, 51
Agency services for other Government Departments, 91
Agriculture, Fisheries and Food, Ministry of, 25, 96
Aliens Order, 1953, 58, 160
Anthrax prevention, 140
Appointed Factory Doctors, 140, 147
Appointments Offices, 43, 53, 68
Appointments service after First World War, 37
Arbitration, 20, 23, 120, 123
Australian Assisted Passage Scheme, 161

Baking Industry (Hours of Work) Act, 1954, 25, 131
Bevin, The Rt. Hon. Ernest, 27, 39, 41, 44, 45, 56, 82, 92, 134, 146, 201
Blind persons, training and employment of, 90
Board of Inland Revenue, agency service for, 193
Board of Trade, 15, 34, 62, 127, 165
Boards of Arbitration, 123, 124
British Association for Commercial and Industrial Education, co-operation with, 133
British Employers' Confederation, 69, 71, 125, 148
British Institute of Management, co-operation with, 133
Brown, The Rt. Hon. Ernest, 45, 201
Business Training Scheme, 47, 51, 69

Careers booklets, 76, 78
Catering Wages Act, 1943, 21, 25, 65, 127
Catering Wages Boards, 128, 131
Catering Wages Commission, 127
Central Statistical Office, 170
Central Youth Employment Executive, 18, 54, 75
Chief Industrial Commissioner, 23, 121, 177
Chief Information Officer, 184, 185
Chief Inspector, 184
Chief Inspector of Factories, 45, 134, 141, 145
Chief Instructions Officer, 184, 185

Civil Liabilities (Resettlement) Scheme, 37
Collective bargaining, 21, 26, 33, 117
Colombo Plan, technical assistance, 53, 68, 157
Commission of Inquiry (Wages Councils), 128
Committee of Inquiry on the Rehabilitation, Training and Resettlement of Disabled Persons, 52
Committees of Investigation, 126
Commonwealth Relations Office, co-operation with, 157
Conciliation, 20, 21, 22, 33, 39, 55, 118, 121
Conciliation Act, 1896, 21, 33, 118, 121, 123, 124, 125, 126
Conciliation Officers, 39, 121
Conditions of Employment and National Arbitration Order, 1940, 46
Conscientious Objectors, Local Tribunal for, 107
Control of Engagement Order, 1947, 68
Cost of Living Advisory Committee, 171
Cost of services provided by the Ministry of Labour and National Service, 186
Courts of Inquiry, 39, 126

Defence, Ministry of, 51, 70
Deferment of call-up for National Service, 20, 42, 105
Demobilisation of the Armed Forces, 46, 47
Demobilisation, industrial, after the 1939–45 war, 46, 48
Department of Agriculture for Scotland, 26, 96
Department of Health for Scotland, agency service for, 192, 194
Department of Scientific and Industrial Research, liaison with, 144
Development Areas, 62
Disabled Persons (Employment) Act, 1944, 17, 44, 52, 82, 88, 92, 203
Disabled persons:
 Designated employment for, 82, 84
 Employment of, 17, 51, 82
 Home-workers, 89

GEORGE ALLEN & UNWIN LTD

London: 40 Museum Street, W.C.1

Auckland: 24 Wyndham Street
Bombay: 15 Graham Road, Ballard Estate, Bombay 1
Calcutta: 17 Chittaranjan Avenue, Calcutta 13
Cape Town: 109 Long Street
Karachi: Metherson's Estate, Wood Street, Karachi 2
New Delhi: 13–14 Ajmeri Gate Extension, New Delhi 1
São Paulo: Avenida 9 de Julho 1138–Ap. 51
Singapore, South-East Asia and Far East: 36c Prinsep Street
Sydney, N.S.W.: Bradbury House, 55 York Street
Toronto: 91 Wellington Street West

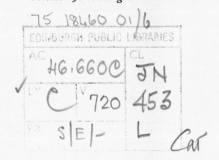